In Defense of the Irrational Peasant

Kusum Nair

In Defense of the **Irrational Peasant**

Indian Agriculture after the Green Revolution

The University of Chicago Press
Chicago and London

For my parents

The University of Chicago Press, Chicago 60637
The University of Chicago Press, Ltd., London

Kusum Nair is the author of *The
Lonely Furrow, Three Bowls of Rice* and
Blossoms in the Dust, a University of Chicago
Press Midway Reprint.

Library of Congress Cataloging in Publication Data

Nair, Kusum.
In defense of the irrational peasant.

Includes bibliographical references and index.
1. Peasantry—India. 2. Farmers—India.
3. Agriculture and state—India. I. Title.
HD1537.I4N33   301.44'43'0954   78-26707
ISBN 0-226-56798-2

Contents

Social structures, types, and attitudes are coins that do not readily melt. Once they are formed they persist, possibly for centuries, and since different structures and types display different degrees of this ability to survive, we almost always find that actual group and national behavior more or less departs from what we should expect it to be if we tried to infer it from the dominant forms of the productive process.

Joseph A. Schumpeter, *Ten Great Economists: From Marx to Keynes* (New York: Oxford University Press, 1969) p. 14.

Preface

It may sometimes be easier to build a million-ton steel plant—with borrowed money and hired know-how, if necessary—than to change a man's outlook on such matters as the use of irrigation water, fertilizer or contraceptives.
Kusum Nair, *Blossoms in the Dust* (London: Gerald Duckworth, 1961), p. xxiii.

The lines were written some twenty years ago, a decade after the first phase of planned development of agriculture in India after independence. The effort has continued. Five Five Year Plans have been completed. This book takes a fresh look at the same agrarian landscape a decade after the most recent phase and development phenomenon generally known as the "Green Revolution." This time nine months were spent in the field in six states—Bihar, Punjab, Uttar Pradesh, Kerela, Tamilnadu and Maharashtra—in districts where new high-yielding varieties of wheat, rice, sorghum, or cotton were being cultivated most extensively.

Aside from the farmers who did or did not adopt the new seeds and the associated technology, ministers, members of the Planning Commission, faculty of the universities and research institutes and administrators involved in or concerned with the formulation of agricultural policy and its implementation were interviewed at every level—federal, state, and district. Originally, in fact, the plan was to write about the policy makers—*their* perceptions of problems and issues pertaining to agricultural growth, technology, employment, and income distribution. I did obtain from them uniquely open and frank interviews. After reviewing the field data, however, I changed my mind and decided once again to write about the farmer, since his role continues to be, not the sole, but the most critical variable in agricultural production. The Green Revolution has not made it any lesser. Nor has it solved the problem of achieving an adequate rate of increasing crop production. The other project remains to be written.

My style again is narrative and descriptive, with most of the statistics in the four appendixes. The theme centers on a single commodity—wheat.

Since the new seeds have been adopted primarily by the "big" farmers with sufficient land, capital, and access to inputs and information, moreover, the study focuses on their performance and response to a new and highly profitable technology and price incentives. Only the first chapter gives a glimpse of the incredible wretchedness and poverty that continue to afflict the lowly, who will continue to be wretched, poor, and irrelevant to commercial production until and unless there is an effective land reform. Small farmers' schemes that have been proliferating like mushrooms in recent years are not an alternative—only a deceptive escape from harsh reality.

Detailed analysis is limited to a comparison between the wheat-growing areas in two states, of Bihar and the Punjab, and three principal case examples—all farmers. Only their names have been changed. As in my previous works, the interviews were unstructured. Notes were taken verbatim and are reported in the raw.

The reader may wonder how three profiles could depict the behavioral types and patterns of some 72 million farm households. Hopefully, he or she will be pleasantly surprised, and will also discover new insights and answers to some unanswered questions. As for example, why has agriculture in the Punjab prospered better than in many states like Bihar, with as good or even richer natural resources?

My recommendations for a new policy emerge from this and twenty years of continuous research on the same problem—of inducing radical changes in the production practices of cultivators in a family type of farming system. As in the past, some readers will be infuriated by this transgression of the sanctum of theory and dogma by plain facts, empirical and historical. They will be angered by my questioning the usefulness or relevance of the concept of economic rationality to the process of change in agriculture.

Max Planck, the originator of the quantum theory in physics, once said that science makes progress funeral by funeral—the old are never converted by a new doctrine; simply replaced by a new generation. In the social sciences it often takes several generations to dislodge obsolescence. In the meantime, serious mistakes can be, and are made, hurting the lives of millions of hapless people. In poor countries, like India and Pakistan, the mistakes can be costly. And the funerals premature and unnecessary—funerals, not of social scientists, who usually operate from a secure haven, but of the designated beneficiaries of development policies formulated on the basis of faulty premises and paradigms.

Acknowledgments

It would be impossible to acknowledge fully the debts accumulated over the past five and a half years to individuals and institutions that made this venture possible.

The initial and major burden for financing the project, including the field research and travels to and within India, was borne by the Food Institute of the East West Center. I am deeply grateful to Chancellor Everett Kleinjans, and more especially, to Nicolaas Luykx, then director of the institute, for making it possible, as well as for his personal encouragement and interest in the work. In addition, I cherish fond memories of Fannie Lee Kai, the administrative assistant, who, aside from raising beautiful orchids which she shared with me, had the unusual verve and talent for making life easier by subverting bureaucratic rules and procedures which afflict academic institutions as much as any others. And of Thammanun Pongsrikul, the smiling, hard-working graduate assistant whose help was invaluable.

But time ran out. The Center's grant could not be stretched beyond three years. And the manuscript was not yet finished. Thanks to Edgar Owens, however, an AID grant enabled me to spend one more year at the Food Institute.

And again, time ran out. And the manuscript was not finished. And so, the Adlai E. Stevenson Center at the University of Chicago came to my rescue and provided sustenance and shelter for another year. I moved to Chicago. My sincere thanks for making it possible go to Chauncy D. Harris, Philip M. Hauser, Milton B. Singer, Ralph Nicholas and the Committee on Southern Asian Studies.

The final revision and version of the manuscript was completed at the Columbia campus of the University of Missouri. Between Chicago and Missouri, in the fall of 1977, I spent about six rewarding weeks living and working in the home of my daughter and son-in-law, Aruna and Barry H. Michie, both on the faculty of Kansas State University in Manhattan.

I am deeply grateful for the unfailing assistance and cooperation I received from the federal and state governments and local officials in India. Also to several staff members of international agencies in New Delhi, such as the World Bank, Ford Foundation, and UNICEF, for their hospitality and manifold courtesies.

A gift of several books on South Asia from N. G. Barrier, at the University of Missouri, was much appreciated.

I do not know how to acknowledge the intellectual contributions of individuals in this country and in India, who willingly gave time for lengthy interviews and discussions, or read various drafts of the manuscript and made valuable suggestions. It would be easy to list a galaxy of luminaries that I am privileged to know and have access to. But that would be unfair to people whose names would mean nothing to nobody. The latter constitute the majority and made the major contribution to the empirical and substantive content of the book. I am equally indebted to both groups—the peasants and professors.

That for so many years now, so many distinguished American universities and institutions have so generously supported the research efforts of a freethinking, footloose hobo like me, is a tribute to the intellectual tolerance and climate in this country that I greatly admire and am thankful for. An official letter to the Internal Revenue Service certified that during the year at Harvard in 1967, I had done absolutely no work for the university—only my own research and writing. It was the same at the East West Food Institute. And at the University of Chicago. What more could anyone ask for? Or deserve?

Introduction

The variety-fertilizer complex has demonstrated its power to break old methods of agriculture . . . . Much of the power of new varieties with fertilizer to launch the development process arises because . . .when pri-vate economic returns are attractive, to the extent that they can make effective personal decisions, cultivators will adopt new practices, use new inputs, and invest their own capital in farming.[1]

It was the gospel. The key policy premise of agricultural strategy in the mid-sixties. In the following decade, economic returns on the cultivation of high-yielding varieties, like Mexican wheat, were extremely attractive in India. And in areas endowed with alluvium soils, medium to high rainfall, and infrastructure, of communications, markets, and services, the larger landowners enjoyed a virtually unrestricted autonomy and freedom of choice from a wide range of production possibilities. They adopted the new seeds readily. But there were wide variations between and, often, within regions, in the efficiency with which they were cultivated—in husbandry, investments, and utilization of land and inputs. Agricultural growth varied accordingly. Between 1962–65 and 1971–74, for instance, crop production increased at a compound rate of 8.35 percent and yields at 4.66 percent per annum in the Punjab, and at 1.67 percent and 0.84 percent, respectively, in Bihar.[2]

Since all economic behavior is assumed to be rational, governed by a criterion of optimization, however, regional differences in rates of investment and growth have been attributed to situational constraints and factor differences in "farm size, quality of land and other factors like irrigation facilities."[3] That is, if the production conditions in the Punjab "were universal in the country as a whole, or even in the irrigated tracts, the miracle in food production anticipated in the mid-sixties could have happened."[4]

Removal or minimization of differences in the environment, conditions and constraints under which farmers operate, became, therefore, a logical and dominant concern of national policy and programs of agricultural development.

Thus, late sowing was found to be partly responsible for low yields of paddy in several areas, especially in the northeast. And so, "to help farmers take up timely planting of rice, a pilot program of raising 'community nurseries', and supply of seedlings to farmers for transplanting at the proper time," was undertaken as a centrally sponsored scheme in important rice-growing states.

So too with the persistent problem of wastage of valuable farmyard manurial resources that the soil sorely needs and cost nothing to compost except the farmer's labor. Again, the solution was sought in a government scheme to launch a comprehensive program "to *conserve, process* and *supply*" rural (and urban) composts to cultivators, presumably bagged and labeled.[5]

It is curious, but never, or rarely, is the question asked whether the government, *any* government, can ever expect to have the resources or administrative capacity to identify and remove all such constraints on production—to equalize and create conditions of optimization on every farm?

The scenario of thousands of earnest little bureaucrats raising rice seedlings with tender care, and then rushing them to each of the millions of paddy cultivators at the right moment for transplanting, is an appealing but manifestly absurd fantasy, fitting for a Gilbert and Sullivan operetta.[6]

Yet another related, but important question rarely asked, is whether there are sufficient and valid reasons for inordinately large disparities in the factors of production between regions with similar soils, climate and crops?

According to one estimate, for example, close to 75 percent of the inter-state variance in rates of agricultural growth in recent years can be explained by the differential in the increase of irrigation.[7] This is plausible, for apart from reducing risk of crop failures significantly, irrigation enables multiple cropping and liberal application of fertilizers. Besides, even in regions with a high rainfall, the yields of *all* irrigated crops are substantially higher than if grown under rain-fed conditions.[8]

During 1962–72, however, new wells representing predominantly private investment of farmers were responsible for over two-thirds of the increase in area under irrigation in the country as a whole. In which case, if we limit our sample to two states in the Indo-Gangetic plain, in 1972, Punjab had a considerably larger area under canal irrigation; lower water rates; scantier supplies of groundwater, at greater depths; and only about half the total area under cultivation than Bihar. Yet wells, of all description, were irrigating over two and a half times more land in the Punjab. Why? The striking difference in farmers' attitude toward well irrigation (as also in the utilization of water from public irrigation works), moreover, has remained basically the same for a century now, in spite of several radical and similar changes having occurred in both regions in the intervening years—in crop varieties, cultural techniques, terms of trade, tenurial regulations, forms of government, and secular institutions for providing credit, information and inputs.

Again, what conceivable factor differences or constraints could account for the entire state of Bihar using only half the quantity of chemical fertilizers on a cropped area of more than 10.5 million hectares than the single small district of Ludhiana (Punjab) did in 1974 on less than 5.5 thousand hectares? By then, Bihar also had 2,550,000 hectares under the new high-yielding seeds of wheat, rice, and maize, which require much larger applications of chemical nutrients than the traditional varieties.

The conventional explanation for the poor performance of agriculture in Bihar is its higher density of population—5,695 per thousand hectares of cultivated land compared to 3,302 in the Punjab. Close to 80 percent of the cultivators in Bihar own two hectares or less. They are not expected to have the capacity to purchase chemical fertilizers or to sink private wells. Yet, precisely because they have so little, of anything, peasants in this category of land size and income do not determine the rates of investment and growth in agriculture. They are practically irrelevant to commercial crop production.

But the remaining 20 percent of the farm households in Bihar are not poor, nor powerless. They own almost 80 percent of the state's rural assets. And although only 5.99 percent of the farmers operate holdings of five hectares and more each, in the aggregate, they cultivate more land than the total net sown area in the Punjab. The latter state, moreover, also has its share of the small and marginal, the poor and rich cultivators. Concentration of rural wealth is, in fact, higher in the Punjab.[9]

And so, if the majority of the larger landowners in Bihar did not obtain nearly as much output from the same basic set of production factors as their counterparts in the Punjab, even during the green years of the varietal revolution, when profits were extremely attractive, it was obviously not due to resource constraints not within their power to overcome. As the reader will discover, it was because they chose not to. And they had the freedom. To choose. Even to be grossly inefficient.

It also follows, however, that most of the production choices of farmers in one of the two states were, wholly or largely, irrational. They could not be so different and yet "rational" according to the "frigid" calculus of economics.

Defenders of the Faith will disagree. They will argue that the differential response to similar production opportunities and alternatives in Bihar, Punjab, or wherever, is in fact entirely rational. The definition of the word "rational" is at fault; misconstrued. Not the farmers' behavior. Thus, if an apparently profitable opportunity to a worker or household is not exploited, economic theory "does not take refuge in assertions about irrationality, contentment with wealth already acquired, or convenient ad hoc shifts in values (i.e., preferences). Rather it postulates the existence of costs, monetary or *psychic,* of taking advantage of these opportunities that eliminate their profitability—costs that may not be easily 'seen' by outside observers." (Italics added.)[10]

In other words, the farmer's goal may not be to maximize merely his crop output. He is maximizing his own satisfaction or utility function, determined by relative prices and resources, as well as a multiplicity of other variables—nonmonetary, invisible perhaps, and partly peculiar or unique to the individual. The decisions units may not even be conscious of their efforts to maximize. Or able necessarily to articulate the "reasons for the systematic patterns in their behavior."[11]

This comprehensive definition of rationality has the merit of providing a simple, consistent, and appealing explanation for understanding not just the economic, but *all* human behavior—from production to procreation. If valid, there is no "irrational" allocation or use of resources by farmers in any region or society, modern or traditional. Nor is a child born of an uncalculated coitus. Of pure passion. As indeed many demographers argue.

But then, of what empirical utility is the concept of "rationality?" How is it even relevant to the developmental process any more than several other universal traits of the human species? Such as intelligence? Or the ability to communicate, which has often resulted in the emergence of a distinct language or dialect across almost every ditch and fossil ridge? The concept loses its operational meaningfulness as an instrument for engineering vast and complex changes in the production behavior, practices, or structure of an agrarian society. No public policy formulated on the rationality assumption so defined could possibly cater to some 70 million bundles of individual "satisfaction" and utility functions of the farm households in India, for instance, with even reasonable predictability. In the absence of a critical measure of unanimity on ends, moreover, whatever the monetary prices and costs, the marginal utility of each input and technique may still be different for every cultivator. Their responses will vary accordingly, to identical shifts in profit and opportunity—except to the extent that common norms, values, and practices are institutionalized by custom, community, or state. Such, in fact, has been the overriding, but largely ignored, lesson of the postwar development strategies.

But then again, if the rationality assumption is dropped, what would the planners in the developing countries outside the socialist bloc substitute for it? The counter proposition, that human behavior is "irrational," or "nonrational," would be even more wrong. Neither true nor functional.

Nor are the policymakers ready for such a momentous change in received theory or their own thinking. Within a decade of its birth, they were writing obituaries for the Green Revolution. They were critical of many of its key assumptions and the euphoric promises of an "abundance" that did not materialize. But faith in the absolute rationality of the peasant-cultivator remained untainted. As reaffirmed by authors of the Asian Agricultural Survey 1976: "The rate of progress is not constrained by the attitudes of farmers . . . . It has been demonstrated that 'tradition-bound' peasant farmers in Asia respond favorably to technical innovations, provided that these are profitable and feasible given the constraints under which the farmers operate."[12]

Any suggestion to the contrary would be regarded as an insult, especially to the non-Caucasian poor.

And yet, actually, the debate and the issue are almost totally irrelevant to the core problems of agricultural development. All farmers, everywhere, are "rational." So what?

Needed is an entirely different approach based on empirically proven premises and recognition of (a) the infinite diversity of factors that determine expressed behavior; and (b) the fact that the sociopsychological (and metaphysical) environment under which farmers live and work can never be cleansed of all constraints, especially in large heterogenous societies. It cannot be done.

In which case, however, in order to create the requisite attitudinal consensus, will it not be necessary to abandon the family farm and its freedoms?

The answer is no. The family type of farming need not be abandoned. Nor the market.

But instead of trying to orchestrate appropriate responses to national needs, priorities, and programs, by juggling the monetary incentives, the strategy would be to use the conventional market mechanisms, prices and taxes, to make it reasonably profitable, but also economically imperative at least for landowners who have the basic resources to cultivate the soil intensively and efficiently, even if the environment is not ideal—under less-than-optimal conditions. It would make it too costly, for instance, uneconomic, for them *not* to sow on time; *not* to dig wells and on-farm ditches for irrigation and drainage; *not* to water and fertilize the soil adequately—that is, *not* do all they can to maximize crop yields and yet survive as farmers and retain possession of the land.

Inevitably, in terms of the socioeconomic and psychic parameters of individual satisfaction and utility, the strategy would require the cultivator to do the "irrational" if need be. But for that regrettable loss of personal freedom—the choice to be rich but inefficient; to own land and not produce all it can—there is no alternative. It may sound Machiavellian to some. But such restraints on liberty and behavior of the individual are not only legitimate, but routine, in every modern profession and organized sector of the economies of the free world. In fact, the regulations are far more stringent and better enforced in the developed-rich democracies than they are in most poor countries under even authoritarian regimes—on farmers and manufacturers; butchers and grocers; automobile drivers and pedestrians; public servants and university professors.[13]

Why then is it regarded as moral and mandatory to accord special dispensation, license, and freedom from all restraints and responsibility, to the "tradition-bound" peasants of India and other developing countries struggling to modernize agriculture?

Are peasants more "rational" than the rest of humanity?

One

The Landless

North India today lay reeling
under the bone-chilling cold wave
which has claimed 227 lives, reports
PTI. *The Times of India,* New
Delhi, December 28, 1973.

PATNA, *January 16—As the
mercury today fell to 5.1 degrees
C—the lowest of the season—the toll
in the cold wave sweeping Bihar
mounted to 215 ....* PTI. *The
Times of India,* New Delhi,
January 17, 1974.

JANUARY 1974—In the plains of north Bihar:

At the edge of a windswept field, the solitary figure of a
child, perhaps three years old, naked but for a pink bangle
around her tiny wrist....

In the garbage heap outside a wayside tea stall, two little
girls not yet in their teens sift the ashes for fragments of
partially burnt wood or coal. The shop boy shoos them away.
Like scared rabbits, they run. But return, to be driven away
again and again....

Everywhere, in the fallows and pastures, toddlers collect
animal dung, twigs, dead leaves. Kids, barely older, stuff
them into sacks or baskets, and carry the load on their heads.
Unsteady bare feet in single file on twisting dirt trails....

The sun has set. Under the black sky, a shriveled old woman
crouches, huddling by a smokey smoldering fire. Wrapped only
in a scanty rag that was once a coarse cotton sari, with every
shivering breath she mumbles, "it is cold. It is very cold"....

In village Kharyia, Shyamlal Biswas, pale, gaunt, with big
anxious eyes, has returned after a day's work on a road under
construction, digging and carrying earth. He earned one
rupee.

Because they are *Gangais* by caste, Shyamlal's wife does not

1

work ouside the home to supplement his earnings. And there is no other adult male in the family. She would not work even on their own farm, that is, if they had one. They do not, however, own any land. Shyamlal is an agricultural wage laborer. But farm work was not available today. January is a lean month.

He wears a short *dhoti*. Part of it is draped over bare shoulders, with one end rolled into a bundle which Shyamlal clutches carefully. It holds four sweet potatoes, four small white potatoes, and two tiny onions. Purchased from the day's income, they will provide supper for his wife, mother, three girls, and himself. An infant son is breast-fed.

The sweet potatoes will be boiled, and the others cooked into a *tarkari* with onions, for which he has bought four annas worth of vegetable oil. It barely fills a third of a six-inch bottle, but will have to suffice for cooking more than one meal. There will be no cereal, bread, or rice tonight.

What about tomorrow?

"I hope I can get some rice on loan from the *bania*," he replies softly. "We will eat it with salt and red pepper." He does not know if he will be hired to work on the road the next day.

Shyamlal's hamlet is over a furlong away from the center of the main village, linked by a footpath, rough and narrow. The family lives in one small room. There is no light. He borrows a lantern. The room has no doors. No furniture of any description. There is one cracked clay pot and a *chakki*. No bedding, not even straw to sleep on.

"We huddle together on the bare floor here, in this corner. We have nothing to cover with. Sometimes we can get some straw."

There is a small bundle of straw by the entrance. It will be used for cooking the evening meal. The *chula* is outside, in a common yard. It is not lit. Shyamlal's wife has been waiting all day for him to return with something to cook.

Most of the wives in this district of Purnea, including those willing to work for a wage, have been waiting helplessly all day this January for their men to return with something to cook. For, like Shyamlal, they are landless and perforce subsist wholly or mainly on casual earnings from casual labor performed for the fortunate few who own most of the arable land.

"We will light the *chula* after the men return. They will purchase something on the way home. Who knows what it will be. We will cook only if they bring something, whatever it is."

What about the children?

"They will eat when we eat. The same food. What else? We have nothing in the house to give them."

As the shadows lengthen, infants cling to their mothers, crying; cold and hungry. As for the dwellings of these *banihars* or day laborers, they are built

> . . .with a bamboo framework, walled in with mats made of reeds, and thatched with *ulu* grass. Such houses consist of a single room, measuring from 10 to 12 feet in length, and from 6 feet to 8 feet wide, having a pent roof called a *doch-hapra*. . . . They have no windows, and the only means of entrance is a doorway closed by a loose mat formed of grass, secured by strips of bamboo. The walls are plastered on the inside with clay.[1]

Taken from the District Gazetteer of 1911, it is an accurate description of the homes of the landless rural population of Purnea in 1974. They have not changed. And not just the housing.

When the British first came to Purnea, "they found the land alluvial, plentiful and the population sparse."[2]

The district must have been surplus in rice, as attested by John Pagan, an Englishman who had settled in Purnea as farmer and merchant. In a letter to J. Duncan, Resident at Benares, he mentions that in a single year (1789–90) rice worth 125,000 rupees was sold in the neighboring state of Nepal. In spite of rich agricultural resources, surplus production of foodgrains, and several high-value cash crops, however, Francis Buchanan discovered in 1809–10 that a "large proportion of the farmers are in debt, chiefly to merchants of various kinds who make advances for their produce, silk, indigo, grain and butter."[3]

Some seventy years later, another historian, W. W. Hunter, affirms that the profit of labor of Purnea's cultivators "eventually goes into the coffers of the lenders of money and grain." Regarding the tenurial situation, he observes: "the Collector estimates that occupancy tenants do not form more than a quarter of the peasantry of the district." As for those entitled to protection from enhancement of rent under Act VIII of 1869, he would say "that no more than one-fourth of the occupancy *rayats* come under this class."[4] Nor was he aware of any small proprietors owning, occupying, and cultivating their hereditary lands without either a *zamindar* above them or a subholder or laborer under them, on revenue-paying as well as revenue-free land.

Among tenants, "a chronic state of poverty" and almost universal indebtedness prevailed, although "rents here are low, some times nominal and *always light in relation to the capabilities of the land.*" (Italics added.) Apparently, there was no rack-renting, "owing to the vast area of cultivable soil that is still available for settlement."[5]

As for the laboring classes, Hunter records that whereas in 1788 their average earning was one rupee or two shillings a month, by 1877, agricultural laborers were being paid 7s. a month.[6]

Unlike his counterpart two centuries ago, Shyamlal earned one rupee in a day instead of in a month. Nevertheless, for the now vastly increased population of nonoccupancy tenants and landless farm workers in Purnea, as in housing, other conditions of life also remained essentially unchanged.

A district collector reportedly once remarked, "The Purnea *rayat* lives, and that is all."

That was in the 1870s.

A hundred years later, and almost a decade after the Green Revolution, *they still lived. That is all.*

Special inquiries regarding the condition of the people were made in 1888. According to the report:

> ... if the condition of the people is not better, it is not due to their wanting opportunity .... *The people of Purnea are for*

the most part wanting in effort or desire to improve themselves. They have learnt to be content with such things as they have; they will not even, when in want, accept good wages if it involves leaving their homes and working a little more than they are accustomed to . . . . Though the Chotanagpur or Dhangar coolies pass through the district in hundreds every year, voluntarily going to Darjeeling in search of employment, no Purnea cooly was ever known to do so.[7] (Italics added.)

On the contrary, unskilled labor had to be imported from the west and south for hard manual work on the farms, as well as for construction of roads and railways.

The alleged lack of "inclination to improvement," found confirmation in another inquiry conducted along with the *Survey and Settlement Operations* (1901–8). Though the population was still sparse and land was plentiful, according to L. S. S. O'Malley: "Instances were not unknown during the settlement of men, who held small pieces of land and cultivated with borrowed bullocks on produce rents, utterly refusing to accept *parchas* or *khatians* for them as they said they could live much more comfortably as ordinary labourers earning 4 to 8 annas a day in addition to their food."[8]

And then again, in 1960, according to yet another survey of village Rampur Kodarkati in the Araria subdivision of Purnea district: "The majority of labourers was landless. *The average type of labourers was found to be half-starved due to their allergy to work even if work was easily obtainable.* It was remarkable that they should have apathy to work in the Kosi canal which is under construction within a furlong from the village."[9] (Italics added.)

The revised District Gazetteer of Purnea by P. C. Roy Chaudhury (1963) reiterates the charge that the "local labourers are rather lethargic and have an allergy to work. The local labourers, it is said, prefer to remain half starved than to work to the full of their capacity." Hence, although "The percentage of cultivating labourers to the total agricultural population in the district of Purnea is about more than 25 per cent . . . *the paddy crops of Purnea might not be cut if labourers from other districts do not come to Purnea.*"[10] (Italics added.)

To what could the apparent "constitutional indolence" of Purnea's labor be attributed?

The commonest explanation has been the climate. Though Hamilton's East India Gazetteer (1815) describes the district as a fertile, well-watered flat, O'Malley states that "the greatest mortality is caused by fevers . . . . The prevalence of fever, and especially malarial fever, is moreover, not of recent date." O'Malley quotes "a common proverb" that is still current:

Na zahar khao, na mahur khao.
Marna hai, to Purania jao. [11]

Whatever the reason for "listlessness and apathy" among Purnea-born farm workers, one of its consequences was an influx of immigrants from other districts. By 1921 they constituted 10.8 percent of Purnea's total population.

Among the immigrants, a major group to settle in the district as landless laborers and sharecroppers consists of Santhals. They came, or were brought by the large landlords and indigo planters, mostly from the Santhal Parganas and Chotanagpur area because of a reputation for robust health and "a tremendous capacity to work in hot summer or shivering winter." The reputation has not diminished. Farmers still prefer to employ Santhal labor.

Two questions, however, remain unanswered. Why was the vitality of the Santhals in Purnea not sapped by the debilitating climate and malaria? Secondly, in spite of hard work and preference in the job market, why have they remained as poor, possibly poorer, than the allegedly lazy non-tribal labor in the district?

In the winter of 1974, like Shyamlal and the rest, the Santhals also are barely managing, somehow or other, just to live. Their staple diet consists almost entirely of dehydrated sweet potato. Their windowless huts are empty of furniture, food, and clothing. And the people: gaunt and emaciated. Men, unshaven, shirtless. Handsome women. Black eyes, unsmiling, nervous, suspicious. Children everywhere, of all ages. Babes tugging at sagging breasts. Infants, crawling, walking, stumbling. Thin dark bodies, naked, or in rags hanging by the shoulder. Bare bottoms, bare feet, distended bellies. They stand around. Sprawl on the grass. On the back of a grazing buffalo. Vacant looks. Puzzled . . . .

"Yes, there is a primary school near by. Yes, it is free."

Why are the kids not in the school then? Is it a holiday today?

"No, it is not a holiday. But how can they go to school in this condition? They are hungry. They have no clothes. No food. How can they concentrate if the stomach is hurting from hunger?"

Two

Bir Babu—The Landlord

If in a hundred years or more, the landless farm workers of Purnea, lethargic and hardworking, managed only and barely "just to exist," how about the more fortunate who owned land in 1974 and earlier?

As a result of the several "revolutionary" measures adopted by the state government since independence, "history is being made in the district of Purnea on the anvil of land reforms covering . . . land redistribution, ceiling on existing holdings, consolidation of holdings and co-operative farming." Since the principle objective was to bring about a socialistic pattern of society:

> . . . the landed community either the *zamindars* or the large scale cultivators had to be touched . . . . in Purnea district there are quite a few cultivators with thousands of acres of cultivable land—an unique feature in Bihar . . . . *The type of village structure before the abolition of zamindari was introduced has been on the decline. . . . In the present picture the great house of zamindars has disappeared.* (Italics added.)

That was written by a loyal civil servant in 1963.[1] Not so in Damdaha, however, a *thana* in Purnea district. Even a decade later, the "picture" here closely resembles the description by O'Malley in 1911: "the type of a truly pastoral country, where hardy Rajputs and others have, from generation to generation, devoted themselves to agricultural pursuits . . . ."[2] More im-

8

portantly, "the great house" of the local *zamindar* has not
disappeared.

"We are of Rajput caste. Our forefathers came here from
another province."

Where?

"From the Central Provinces. Oh, a long time ago. Must be
a hundred years or so."

How come? That is a long distance from here.

"As you know, it is a tradition in our caste to go wherever
there is a good match for marriage . . . ."

Just for marriage?

"That is so. We are told, that our forefathers—it must have
been my great-grandfather—came here. At that time, the river
Kosi was very troublesome, and it was difficult to move
around, to travel. So the family just stayed here."

Did you bring in the Santhals?

"Yes. This Kosi area was all a jungle then and the population was sparse. That is why we brought the Santhals. We
brought them from the Santhal Parganas, to reclaim the land
for cultivation. They are hardy. They had nothing when they
came. We had too much land. We settled them here."

And so by 1921: "The high grass jungle described in the
report of 1891 has now become one of the most fertile and best
cultivated areas in the district, and Damdaha is now with the
exception of Katihar the most densely populated tract in the
sub-division."[3]

Bir Babu, the head of this pioneering family, is in his late
sixties, gray, in a brown woollen shirt and *dhoti*—socks, slip-
pers, two fountain pens in the breast pocket. His voice is loud
and strong and he speaks in Hindi mixed with English words
and phrases in a pronounced Bihari accent.

How big was your *zamindari*?

"We were not *zamindars* originally. In fact, our forefathers
must have been quite poor. But as they made money, they
purchased land—gradually, in bits and pieces. The *zamindari*
also was accumulated slowly, over time. They purchased
zamindari rights whenever and wherever they could. Land in
those days was considered a good investment. People thought
that the best thing to do with their savings was to purchase

land. That is what happened. We bought land. We did not get it all in one place, however."

How much land did you have finally?

"We had eight to ten thousand acres under *direct* cultivation. That is our own. The *zamindari* estate was much bigger. It spread over in other districts also. In Bhagalpur district we had a lot of land. Cultivation, agriculture, has been our main occupation."

He pauses as tea and sweets are brought in for refreshment.

"And now. And now," he says with an anguished expression, "at one stroke the government has taken away everything, *everything*. Everything is gone."

This is true. The *zamindari* is gone; the whole system. And a ceiling has been imposed on agricultural holdings at an infinitesimally lower level than the eight or ten thousand acres once owned by Bir Babu. His ancestral home, however, has by no means disappeared. And like the grass huts of the laborers, it too is exactly like the *"deorhis* of the larger landed proprietors or *zamindars"* of Purnea, described by O'Malley some sixty years ago. As then, "the best room in the house," where we sit, is furnished "in the European style with sofas, arm-chairs, mirrors, and pictures."[4] The portraits on the walls are of family and friends. Aside from plastic flowers and a medley of artifacts of indifferent taste, the radio set is a modern intrusion. So also, the flush toilet in the bathroom.

Surrounded by a high wall with heavy iron gates, the three-storied complex still dominates the absolutely flat landscape. For miles around, as far as the eye can see, it is the only house of brick in an ocean of grass, bamboo, and straw—clusters of low thatched huts, submerged or seemingly afloat in the gray morning mist.

Pervasive as the winter mist also is the presence and influence of Bir Babu himself in Damdaha and beyond. Reportedly the biggest landowner in the district, in spite of the recent "revolutionary" reforms, he is alleged to own several thousand acres. No one, including the state government, appears to know how much for sure. For Bir Babu personally, in fact, the transition to the present order may have been a wrench, but not a total or even a drastic break with the past. Nevertheless, the nostalgia lingers.

"See that photo on the wall, of Rajendra Babu with our family when we were children? Gandhijee also came here and stayed with us in this humble cottage. My father was alive then. We were loyal nationalists and very well known. When Pandit Nehru came in 1937, to campaign for the general election, I took him around in the district. And then, in the middle of nowhere, on the road, one wheel of my car fell off. I was so embarrassed. I had to appeal to the police car that was trailing us to help us out . . . .

"Politically, we were against the government then; antigovernment. But you know, we enjoyed more respect and honor under the British administration than we do now, under this *swaraj*. The quit-India movement in 1942 was quite strong here. Sivaraman, who is in the planning commission now, was our collector at the time. Whenever there was a problem, unrest among the people, he would consult me: 'Bir Babu what should we do?' he would ask."

How much land do you have now?
"Now?" He hesitates, but only momentarily. "I don't want to tell lies. But the land that I had mentioned earlier, the eight to ten thousand acres, that is all gone. It is gone because our government made a settlement survey here. During the survey, our Santhal *bataidars* who used to cultivate the land and take a share of the produce—it was as much to their advantage as ours—well, they were told to make claims to the land they were cultivating. Whatever they claimed became theirs. Since that day, my animals cannot graze in that land. I get no share in its income. I cannot even enter those fields. We have surrendered all claims. That is how I lost it."

But then, he goes on to confess, "Since I was in the Council in Patna for twenty years, I saw the trends; the writing on the wall. And, of course, when a man sees a storm approaching, he prepares for it. Who will stay inside the house if he fears that it will be blown away in the storm?"

Who indeed?
"I am telling you the truth. This was the situation. So, when I saw what was coming, I began to sell the land. I sold it for 200, 250, 300, 400 rupees an acre—at whatever price I could get. And I kept on selling. Of course, I had a deep

attachment to the land. All our sustenance came from it. Nevertheless, I kept selling. That is how we lost most of our land."

In other words, *most* of it was sold and not surrendered to the *bataidars*.

"Of what was left—that land—some was given to my relations. I transferred it to their names. That is the truth. Now our ministers are going around searching for it. 'This man is a thief,' they say. 'Bir Babu has stolen the land; he has hidden it.'"

A flicker of a smile betrays the satisfaction he feels at having outwitted the government.

Do you give your land to sharecroppers any more?

"*Nai. Nai.* No more sharecropping any more. We do not give *any* land on *batai* now. The result is that the poor are suffering."

With touching conviction he reiterates: "*bataidari* was not a bad system. When we gave land to a poor man on *batai,* we provided the seed. We gave the capital, all the cost of cultivation. If he had any problems—if someone in his family was hungry—*we* helped. To me, my *bataidar* was like a son. The government has stepped in only now. In those days he had no one but us to turn to. We were the social guardians, and perfect guardians. Yes, *perfect*. That is why no one suffered. Now if a man needs help, he has to go to a government office. After endless trips, he may get a loan for, say, one hundred rupees. Out of that 25 rupees will be lost on the way. He would actually receive only 75 rupees, and even that after how much hassle. But then, that is the law now. Whoever cultivates the land becomes its owner."

So, how much land do you still have?

"At present? I think . . . I think I must have maybe three to four hundred *bighas*. That would be about 200 acres. But that is not in my name only—it includes my family members. The whole family."

Presumably, "family" does not include the relatives mentioned earlier, who were given an unspecified acreage. "What I transferred to the *other* relations is gone. They may or may not return it. *I* have made a legal transfer, through a legal document. The registrar has certified that the land has been paid for. I now depend entirely on their sense of honor. As long as they give us its produce, it is all right. The day they refuse, I am helpless. I have made the commitment. Even so, our government is not satisfied. Officials have been ordered, I understand, to find out how much and which of my land is *benami*. I do not know what will happen. The legal aspect is complex. I do not know. In my view, there is no such thing as a *benami* transfer. Where has this word *benami* come from?"

He is hurt. Indignant.

"Now take the example of my daughter and son-in-law. He is a very senior official. Yes, he was secretary of agriculture. My daughter is married to him. I have transferred some land in their names. Now they live in Delhi. If I do not manage their land and crops, who will?"

With a son-in-law as secretary of agriculture, and later a member of the planning commission, how did such policies get formulated in the first place? Who, for example, will gain by the government's scheme to take away the land from you?

"The gain will be that everyone will become a landowner and vote for the government's candidates. This is all a game for winning elections. Nothing else. On the other hand, it is breaking up families—the natural God-given cooperative we had of father, son, and grandson. Now everyone is separate because I have distributed the land. We still live and eat together. But when you come, I have to say, this property is not mine. It belongs to my son."

But you are very influential. With all your highly placed connections, don't you influence government policy?

"How? No one consults me anymore. When I was in the Council, I used to express my views loud and clear. In Shri Babu and Anugrah Babu's time, the land ceiling bill that *we* drafted—you should see that. No one had any grievance against it. That was in 1955. But that bill was never implemented. And from time to time, they keep changing the law—all on paper."

What does your son-in-law have to say with regard to these policies?

"He is retired now. But you are right. I am not applauding him, though I know that on several occasions when these policies were discussed, he did oppose them. It is your Indira

Gandhi who gives orders—'we are not going to remove poverty. *Garibi hatao'*. Can a civil servant say no to the prime minister? Does he have the power? No. He has no voice. He is simply told, 'You will have to do so, and so, and so. I want to remove poverty. Land must be given to every man.'"

The government is anxious about the condition of the poor. Don't you agree that poverty should be removed?

"In today's world only a fool would say no—that the poor should remain poor. Everyone wants to see them progress. But the poor are not a recent creation. They have always been there. You say now that you are getting rid of poverty. I say, on the contrary. You are increasing it. The man who ate rice costing eight annas a seer is now spending two and a half rupees for one seer. Is he less poor or poorer than before? And then, you want to cut me down in order to improve his condition. You want to do it at the cost of my survival? The government has taken away my *zamindari.* It has taken away my land. Has it done any good? Has it made the poor any richer?"

He is angry. Returning to the topic of greater immediacy, however, he repeats the worrisome question concerning *benami* transfers.

"So, as I was saying, where did this word *benami* come from? I claim that I have transferred the land to various people. *I have the freedom to do so. I have every right to do so.* It is *my* land and *my free choice.* It is also the right of the people who have received the land, their choice, if they want to leave it in my custody to cultivate it.

"My regret is not so much the loss of the *zamindari.* The money was there, of course. The real regret is over the loss of other benefits, the privileges and patronage that went with it—the plenty that we shared with people who depended on us. All that is gone as well. Every year I used to give away three to four hundred maunds of fish to friends and others. Now *I* have to purchase fish at ten rupees a kilo. This is the condition that my government has reduced us to. We have become beggars now."

Why, you live well. You have enough to eat?

"Oh yes," he concedes. "We have enough to eat. We have enough land. We cultivate it. We have everything. You see, even if they took away *all* my land, for a very long time to come, my children will not starve. We will not be hurt because we have accumulated a great deal. We have made our profit."

He is more concerned about a decline in agricultural production.

"If you distributed my land among fifty families, for example, all the advantages of scale, of farming it as a single unit, would be lost. Besides, can a cultivator with two or four *bighas* of land, will he use the new scientific ways of cultivation that I am practicing? He will not be able to. He cannot. In which case, will production increase or will it decrease?"

What crops are you cultivating?

"Rice, maize, jute, everything. Everything grows on our land."

Wheat?

"Wheat? Wheat—yes, of course. Wheat does exceedingly well here. This is an excellent area for wheat."

How much wheat do you get in an acre?

"Wheat you see, under the old system we used to get five to ten maunds in one acre. Now, with the new techniques and the improved varieties of seed that have been introduced, I have seen people get as much as thirty maunds! Some get twenty maunds. It all depends on how hard a man works. It also depends on the kind of irrigation facilities he has."

How is your land irrigated?

"We get water from the canal. We also have seven to eight hundred bamboo borings. I find boring is more profitable. We can get water whenever we want it—at midnight or whenever. The canals are dry right now and I need water."

But you must have benefited greatly from the Kosi project?

"There have been gains and there have been losses. The water rate, for example, is very high—for irrigation. A farmer cannot afford it."

How much is it?

"It is too much. We had entertained very high hopes when we got the canal. But due to faulty engineering, perhaps, if I irrigate 100 *bighas* bordering the canal, the adjoining 100 *bighas* also get flooded. This year, I could not harvest the paddy from one such field because the laborers could not enter it. It had so much water."

Do you take only one crop?

"No. We take two crops. But paddy is harvested when there is water in the field. If the land dries quickly after the crop has been cut we can sow the second crop. If it does not dry on time, we cannot take a second crop on the same land."

Have you done something about it?

"Well, I said to the authorities: 'Arrange for the drainage. Take the water out'. But for that there is no provision. I have made repeated complaints in several places. What can I say. It is not good to complain . . . ."

What then are your yields of wheat from the irrigated land?

"On my farm, I don't think we get more than ten or twelve maunds in an acre. Not more."

But why? Are you cultivating the traditional *desi* varieties?

"No. No. Now it is all the new type. *Desi* is practically finished. Cannot find *desi* seed any more even in a village. I wanted to sow some this year, of the old variety. Had to bring the seed from Patna—could get very little. Everyone says the new varieties are better. They give higher yields."

In that case, why do you get such low yields? What is the reason?

"The reason is that those who can personally supervise the cultivation closely—what can I say. Everything depends on the timeliness of various operations. If done on time, the output will increase. If not. It will decrease. I have a lot of difficulties . . . ."

I have not understood. Your son lives here? And how many servants do you employ?

"Servants? There must be a great many. Thanks to the Almighty, I am still giving three, four, five, maunds of rice everyday for their meals. Even if I wanted to get rid of some of them, whom should I send away?"

Yes. But how many do you have?

"The permanent hands at present—they must be close to 150 men. As for daily wage labor—temporary workers that come and go—we hire 200 or 150 at least. They work for us during the day and are paid off the same evening."

Have you mechanized?

"There are 91 tractors in the district. But do you know, they are not used on the farms. You will find them on the road, transporting goods and people—as a conveyance for carrying people. We had a function here last night, and a dozen or so tractors were running around . . . ."

How many do you have?

"I have six tractors. Some are old, from before. Several are out of repair—just sitting. Only two or three are working. But then I have the bullock-drawn plows. We use those for cultivation. And now another difficulty has cropped up. I will not be permitted to keep any pasture land."

How many cattle do you have?

"Now, I don't think we have more than six or seven hundred. But how will I feed them? After all, is it not a national asset? In Hindusthan, cattle are wealth. If we do not take care of the cow, what will our children eat? There will be no milk. No manure. Then there is a calf every year. The male calf is used for the plow. The female provides milk and manure. It makes me very sad. When the government takes away my land, I will be allowed only fifteen acres. Just calculate. In fifteen acres, there will not be standing room even for my animals. Not even standing room."

Nostalgically he recalls: "In my *babujee's* time, we used to have five to six thousand heads of cattle. Why did we need so many? Because we had so much land. By keeping the animals we got natural manuring. And with cow dung we could grow money crops like tobacco, chili peppers, and so on."

That is how it used to be 150 years ago. As described by Francis Buchanan:

> . . . the usual manner of manuring the few fields where any
> such thing is attempted, is for two or three successive
> nights to gather a herd of cattle on a narrow space. This is
> continued in turns, until the whole field receives a scanty
> supply. Tobacco, kitchen gardens, mulberry, and sugarcane
> are generally allowed a little cowdung and ashes, but not in

every place, and everywhere in so scanty a proportion as to produce very little good . . . .[5]

How about chemical fertilizers? Aren't you using fertilizers now?

"Yes. I use fertilizer. But I don't have much confidence in it. We have seen that hyacinth, you know water hyacinth, is very good. It is a very fine method of manuring. It is good and it costs much less. We have started to use chemical fertilizers also, but along with cow dung. Actually, I still use much more of the old type."

What is that?

"The same. Cow dung collected from the animals we own."

Three

Rich but Inefficient

It was accumulated gradually, from the rent and sweat of serf labor. Because they were Rajputs, his forefathers would not have plowed or worked the soil with their hands even when they were poor.

Now the farm is larger than that of 99.5 percent of the farmers in India, the land reforms notwithstanding.[1] He does not therefore, suffer from the innumerable constraints that small and poor cultivators are born to—insufficient land, capital, credit, calories. And unlike them, he is above and beyond the orbit of local traditions, mores, and institutions that might restrict his freedoms of behavior, choice, and action. He is not beholden to the village communities around him. On the contrary. The villagers and even the local officials kowtow to him with a deference fit for royalty. They fear his power and seek his patronage.

And yet, Bir Babu's employment of the factors of production, traditional and modern, is grossly inefficient. He knows it. He is not insensitive to price. And he produces a surplus of grain and cash crops that are marketed commercially. But he makes no ostensible effort to maximize production or profit.

It is not that Bir Babu ever failed to move with the currents of modern technological progress. He owned a car in the 30s, braving such awkward hazards as having its wheels fly off when transporting no less a passenger than the first prime minister of

India. In those days even the bicycle was a novelty in the rural areas.

Now he has adopted the bundle of inputs associated with the latest agricultural technology—seed, fertilizer, tractor, irrigation. Curiously, however, "the new scientific ways of cultivation" have had little or no impact on most of Bir Babu's traditional beliefs and attitudes pertaining to production practices—those beliefs and attitudes remain remarkably unchanged.

He applies chemical fertilizers, for example, but reluctantly. He prefers cow dung. Again, he has several tractors. Some of them were purchased prior to the Green Revolution. Yet most of the machines are out of repair, "just sitting." Maintenance is neglected, one suspects, because he never intended to use the tractor for cultivation. Bullocks continue to plow the land.

And the new seed, heralded as "a seed packed with explosive force . . . shattering much of the old myths, cynicism, and sloth."[2] Like all progressive farmers, Bir Babu has exchanged the old seeds for new. And for a sound economic reason. They give higher yields. Ironically, with a yield of 1100 kg per hectare, however, Bir Babu is producing *less* from the high-yielding Mexican wheat than the potential of the discarded *desi* varieties.

Irrigation is not a modern innovation in Indian agriculture. But aside from the fact that it frequently makes the difference between a crop and no crop at all, it is absolutely essential for the cultivation of the new varieties.

Most of Bir Babu's land is watered by a canal from the river Kosi that wends its wayward way along the western border of the district. Bir Babu uses the water for irrigation, but refuses to invest in drainage, even though he can double crop *only* if the land dries quickly after the paddy has been harvested.

Rice is rotting in the ground this year because too much water prevented the laborers from entering the field to harvest it. Two crops have been lost on that land. Yet Bir Babu's only response has been to complain and request the government to arrange for the drainage.

He loses the crops, investment, and income. But the government must drain his land, since: "They bring us the water . . . ." Compare this to the attitude and behavior of cultivators in a neighboring district fifteen years earlier. Owning two acres or less, they were all ex-tenants of another ex-*zamindar*.

"Every village here has an *ahar*. But it has no water in it because ever since *zamindari* was abolished no one has maintained these tanks and so they have silted up. The result is that if there are no winter showers now our *rabi* crops wither away," explains the *mukhia*.

"Who maintained these *ahars* previously?" I ask.

"The *zamindar's* agent used to get it done. The *zamindar* saw to it that everyone got the irrigation water and so we used to be certain of reaping good harvests. Now it is the government's responsibility, but the government simply passes orders. Nothing gets done," is the reply.

"In Bashaita there are four wells from the time of the *zamindar*," says the representative of that village. "In his time they were being repaired regularly. Now they are all filled up and we have no water. We are suffering terribly."

"What is your plan?" I ask the *mukhia*.

"Please give us a canal," he pleads with folded hands. "For the past three years our crops have been failing regularly." He has no other plan.

"But why do you not repair the wells and *ahars* yourself if the government does not do it, instead of waiting for a canal and letting your crops wither in the meantime? Didn't the *zamindar* repair them with your labour, by compelling you to contribute *begar?* Can't you do the same now of your own free will?"

They—the *mukhia*, members of the *panchayat* and the rest—do not think so. "What are we paying the government taxes for?" they say. "Why should the government not do it?" is the attitude of all. As for *begar* or free labour, which they gave to the *zamindar*—"Oh we did not mind it. We used to be given *chana* and *gud* for lunch, and at least the 'works' were maintained. Now it is the government's responsibility. Why should we do it?"[3]

That was in 1959. They asked: "Why should we do it?" They did not say: "We cannot do it."

Production decisions and control over the land vested entirely with the cultivators now instead of the *zamindar*. They subsisted on the brink of starvation. But rather than maintain the existing sources of irrigation, as they had done for centuries, they chose to risk lower yields and high uncertainty inherent in rain-fed cultivation until such time as the government shouldered the cost and responsibility of providing the water. In the meantime, their crops had failed for three years in succession. They were "suffering terribly," with admirable fortitude.

Though seemingly contrary to common sense, those farmers' choices might have been dictated by a fine calculation of marginal costs and returns. They did not say so. But maybe the yields and prices of their farm products were too low to warrant the voluntary investment of personal labor for desilting the irrigation tanks and wells. It was more rational therefore to let the crops die when it did not rain.

In less than a decade, however, the Green Revolution had swept across the plains of Purnea, Bihar, and India. It revolutionized the economics of grain production, making irrigation extremely profitable. Yet, in spite of the new and unprecedented rates of return, Bir Babu's logic, reasoning, and attitude concerning the worth of crops and irrigation were practically identical with those of the poor, very small, and virtually illiterate peasants. Like them, he will do nothing himself—not even what he can afford—to exploit the available water resources effectively. He too would only complain and, pending action by the administration, suffer repeated crop failures, if necessary.

As pointed out earlier, Bir Babu always responded to investment opportunities and incentives in agriculture predictably and rationally. He readily adopted every modern component of the latest technological revolution.

Unfortunately, however, Bir Babu chose to utilize even the factors most critical to productivity with a poetic license and inefficiency not foreseen by the scientists and strategists of the High Yielding Varieties Program, better known as the Green Revolution. And so, the rich alluvium soil turned into a soggy mire, instead of gold. Beneath the surface modernization of his farm, practically nothing was transformed. For Bir Babu himself remained what he has always been—*rich but inefficient.*

Four

˙ Born to the Profession

In the district of Ludhiana, Mohinder Singh also has adopted "the new scientific ways of cultivation." He obtains an average yield of 4,490 kg per hectare of wheat. Cropping intensity is close to 175 percent.

"I am producing only for seed."

That must be very profitable?

"No; and ye-es," is the cautious reply. "Yes. It can be—is—certainly a paying proposition. But it is a risky business. It is a *very* risky business."

He admits to having cleared a net profit of Rs. 5,000 per hectare, at times. But that, he clarifies, "is only because of this seed production. Also, in calculating the profit, we do not include our own labor, or the cost of risk. As I said, the risk factor is very high. I may make very good money on one crop this year, and lose everything on another."

Besides wheat, Mohinder is growing corn, peanuts, and several types of vegetables, also for seed. It is sold to the National Seeds Corporation, the State Department of Agriculture, and to private seed merchants.

Compared to Bir Babu, Mohinder is a much smaller landowner. He owns less than twenty-four acres. He is operating a unit of 95 acres, however, because it is a joint family venture.

"Father died last year." But the property was not divided. "I personally feel that with bigger size we can have more efficient production. If we divided this, each of the four brothers will have a tractor. It means that we will need four tractors. And for each tractor, we will need all the equipment. Similarly, with combine. And, so on. That alone will make the production cost very high. Even now, my machinery and I are under-employed."

What machinery do you have at present?

"Now? For this four-family unit, we have two tractors—of 35 hp each. One wheat harvest combine. And all the auxiliary implements, such as seed drill, corn planter, harrow, tiller, et cetera. For irrigation, we have four tubewells. Total investment in equipment and the tube-wells would come to about 150,000 rupees."

Car or jeep?

"Yes. Car and a scooter."

You don't use any wage labor then?

"Yes, we do. We have to. The daily average would come to ten workers. That is the average. We need more hands during the rainy season. Otherwise, two are enough."

But why? Don't you work? Or do you just manage the farm?

"Of course I work. I do the sowing and harvesting. Drive the tractor and the combine. We have a tractor driver. But these two operations I do myself—the sowing and harvesting. My brother and I both work. He is a little handicapped. Had polio when he was a child. So he supervises the labor and field operations. Since father's death, my wife keeps the accounts. And mother looks after the female workers. The whole family is involved."

Two brothers are away from home. The eldest, "is taking care of the ancestral property, three miles from here. It is six or seven acres. My youngest brother is in America. He is an engineer. He has a job there."

How many laborers would you need without this mechanization?

"Oh, I think 30 to 40 workers a day. And, several bullocks besides. To maintain the bullocks, I would have to set aside land for growing fodder."

How many do you have now?

"None. There is not a single bullock on this farm. There isn't one in the whole village. Nobody keeps them any more . . . .

"You see, compared to machinery, the cost of working with bullocks is very much higher," he declares with persuasive vehemence. "Some farmers make ill use of machinery. But that is not the fault of the machines. The fault lies in the use of machinery. Provided you use it efficiently; yes, efficiently, then machinery is definitely cheaper."

Mohinder's notion of "efficiency" does not apparently end or coincide with merely the investment in a new, more productive factor. Unlike Bir Babu, moreover, who owns half a dozen tractors but continues to cultivate the land with bullock-drawn plows anyway, when Mohinder changes a tool or technique, he substitutes one for the other. He does not simply add the "new" to the "old" like a decorative overlay.

The attitude is reflected in his life-style as well—to a degree unusual in the countryside. Young, dark, bearded, and handsome in a black turban, on this crisp wintry morning, he is dressed in custom-made clothes—blue slacks, tweed jacket over an open-collared checked shirt, socks, and polished shoes. He is fluent in English. The interview is conducted in English. The inevitable Punjabi syntax and pronunciation, however, are tinged with a curious but distinctly American accent.

Again, contrary to tradition, his mother and unmarried brother live apart in the "old brick house that father built." It is small with a walled-in courtyard. Mohinder's family occupies another single-story house nearby, also on the farm. It is not as imposing as Bir Babu's *deorhi*. But it is all new, with the living room furnished in Western style—sofa set, dining table and chairs, draperies, fancy electrical fittings, television set. Built three years ago, it would be considered "modern" in any upper middle class suburb of New Delhi. Even so, his wife is not satisfied.

"We have only three bedrooms," she complains. "We need four. You see, we have two children, a girl and a boy. They are still very young. But they should have separate rooms. And then, we need a guest room as well."

Like Bir Babu, Mohinder is critical of agricultural policies in general, and those relating to land use, in particular. And he is puzzled.

"I fail to understand why they are doing like this. I don't understand."

But why?

"Because these policies—these policies and reforms—are not, I would say, they are not production oriented." He reflects, fumbles for the right words.

"Our goal must be *efficient* production. That is, we need more production to solve this, our food problem. It has become confused by these reforms. It means that these reforms are not good. They should therefore be abandoned, and replaced by measures that can solve the problem. How long can we cheat the masses by just slogans?"

The logic is forceful. Of classical simplicity.

Will you personally lose any land because of the latest ceiling legislation?

"Me? No. We are just below that. You see, I am not a big farmer. I am big only because we are a joint family."

Unlike Bir Babu, moreover, he is not troubled by any legal complications of *benami* transfers to relatives and friends. Then what is the problem, I ask. And if a man like you is not affected, who is?

"Well, there may be some in other districts of Punjab. But their number would be very small."

For the likes of Mohinder, however, they may not forfeit any land, "but our incentive is killed." Previously, for example, he was interested in purchasing more land. "I wanted to buy. Some inefficient farmers wanted to sell. But I don't want it any more. You will be surprised to know that the price of land is falling now."

Instead of expanding his farm operation, in fact, Mohinder is exploring other avenues for investment. He admits the possibility of ultimately quitting agriculture altogether.

"That is how most good farmers are thinking. Because the future is very uncertain."

That maintenance of *economic* farm units is an absolute imperative for efficient production is a self-evident maxim with Mohinder. It follows that there should be a mandatory floor instead of a ceiling on landholdings.

"Now, most people in this village—I myself—everybody is owning twenty to twenty-five acres. That should be the *lowest* limit. We can produce more and cheaper grain than the five-acre *wallah*. You can see for yourself the difference in the standard of cultivation . . . ."

In any case, the maximum acreage permitted under the law will apply only for the present, for a few years at most. In the very next generation that holding would be automatically fragmented—"reduced to two or three acres per member of that family. It will be chaos."

That may be so, I concede. But the government is also worried about the acute unemployment and social injustice that prevail in the rural sector. How would you reconcile the solution of these problems with that of increasing production?

"Oh, I agree that unemployment is a very big factor. But *this* is no solution—*to give one acre to each man and let him starve.*" With puckered eyebrows, he pauses for effect. "This way the whole country will starve."

He reiterates his awareness of the serious dimensions of rural unemployment. "I know it is a big problem." Land should, nevertheless, remain in the hands of farmers capable of maximizing production. For the rest, "we should try to find some other opportunities, such as industries, and the like. Poultry, for example. Punjab could become a paradise in a few years through this poultry. But the government is not supporting it." As for social justice. That too is important. "But our main goal should be to provide food for everyone. This I think is more important. To give food to the poor and needy at a reasonable price, at a price they can afford—that, I think, is more important, the *real justice* . . . ."

But then, should there be no ceiling on land holdings?

"Yes. The ceiling should be there. *But it should be determined according to a given standard of production.* If a man is cultivating, say, ten acres. Then ten multiplied by fifteen—he should be required to give 150 quintals of grain to the government. *If he fails to do so, he should be deprived of the land. That is what the government should do—decide how much land a farmer can have on the basis of the potential standard of his cultivation."*

If that were so, how much land would you like to own?

"There are many factors. If I produce this seed, which needs close personal attention, maybe 200 acres. But if I produce commercial grains, I can manage 2000 acres perhaps. I could use a bigger combine then," he adds wistfully. "It would be cheaper to run. It all depends. . . . But whatever it is, it should be according to one's capacity."

I understand your emphasis on a production-first policy. Many leading economists will agree with you. An important implication of your argument, however, is that if a portion of the land is taken away from farmers like you, it will not be possible to produce enough food—that agricultural growth will slow down?

"That is, that is what I am telling you," he remonstrates. "Now, suppose I have more than 25 acres. That is, I have five or six acres surplus. You take it away from me, and you give it to another person who is not efficient. Then production will fall. Won't it?

"You see," he continues professorially, "agriculture these days is not that old agriculture. It needs a lot of intelligence—lot of, I mean—integration, and effective utilization of all the inputs. I have to search for this knowledge from all kinds of sources. Now unless we have a special class of farmers who can understand and implement the scientists' directions—those people doing research—that agriculture, the *scientific* agriculture of the future, which will provide the solution to our food problem, it will be killed by these reforms."

Mohinder sees himself as an important link between the scientist and the ignorant and illiterate cultivators. "These uneducated farmers, they cannot understand new technologies. How will they learn? Not by preaching. They are not convinced if I lecture to them at the university. But if they come to the field, they believe what they see. Farmers from nearby villages often come over here and ask all kinds of questions. I tell them. I give them seeds. We should have such efficient farms in every block. If they go, it means you are killing everything. But that is what the government is doing. At the same time, it is spoon-feeding the small farmers—giving them loans, *liberal* loans, tubewells, and all that."

In a neighboring village of about 300 families, for instance, "last year, I am told, every acre was mortgaged to the government for a minimum of 500 rupees. That was the credit only ⋅ from the land mortgage bank and cooperative society—not counting the loans from private sources. This is the way they are being given loans. It is nothing but spoon-feeding."

Are you saying that small farmers will remain inefficient even if they have the necessary credit, tube-well, and so on? The government is trying to make more institutional, and therefore, cheaper credit available to small cultivators in the belief that it would enable them to become more productive. Some will say they are not getting enough. You seem to disagree. Is it because you think that small-scale farming cannot be efficient?

"Well, scale is important. But the more important question is Who will accept five acres? Which *intelligent* farmer, that is, will be attracted by or stick to a five-acre farm?"

What do you mean by "intelligent"? Surplus land will be distributed mainly to landless agricultural laborers, mostly Harijans. Isn't that the policy?

"Yeh. This Harijan program. Again, I do not know what our planners are thinking. Mr. Kairon, our late chief minister, gave five-acre plots to these Harijans, and all the facilities. The land was given to them free or at a nominal price. But after two or three years, they sold it and the land went back to the farmers. Though they made some money on the sale, Harijans were not successful in farming it because farming is not their profession. Ultimately, the land will return to the professional farmer."

But why?

"You see," he explains, "farming is not in everyone's blood. Why are Punjabis known for good farming? Why are Jat Sikhs such good farmers? Why are Jews successful in business? I cannot be a successful businessman. I could not run even a village grocery store. But this, agriculture, is our inheritance—the profession we are born to."

But you are exceptional. You do not represent the majority of the farmers.

"I am exceptional only because, even if I have to borrow money to keep the land and cultivate it, I will do it. I will not part with my land. But those masses, they do not have the same sort of interest or goal in their minds. For me this life is not a burden, as it is to them—that is the difference. They are just born to and die in agriculture. And they keep working because they have no option. But agriculture is in our blood. So, if this land is given to Harijans, I don't think they can manage it."

Does that mean that a Harijan will not or cannot learn to be an efficient farmer simply because he is born a Harijan?

"He can learn, provided he has a viable unit, all the facilities, and what is most important, the *intelligence* and a *taste* for farming." He should not have the land just for the sake of status and prestige of owning it.

I can understand "taste," but what do you mean by "intelligence"? There are stupid Harijans, as well as intelligent Harijans, just as there are stupid Jats and intelligent Jats.

"This intelligence means—by intelligence I mean, the *profession* . . . ."

In other words, he is not referring to random differences in the natural intelligence of individuals, but to the inherited socioeconomic values of a caste or ethnic community—Jat or Jewish. Some value systems are more favorable for good farming than others. They produce better farmers. Furthermore, Harijans are not alone in suffering from this apparent lack of "intelligence" and "taste" for agriculture.

"You see there, on the other side of the road. That land is owned by a very big upper caste farmer whose name I will not mention. Now that land is as good as mine. But he grows only one crop. And he is getting five to six—a maximum of eight—quintals of wheat in an acre—which is the *lowest* one can get. We are getting twenty. The difference is that on the the other side of the road it is India, and on this side it is America.

"So, why should that farmer be allowed to keep the land? That land should not be with him," he affirms without waiting for an answer. "Land should be taken away from such people. At the same time, it should *not* be taken from efficient hands. We should not try to fit square pegs in round holes. But that is what the government is doing. As I told you, I cannot be a good businessman. But I am a good farmer. And I can be a good farmer anywhere in the world."

I can be a good farmer anywhere in the world.

Mohinder is probably right. But for the immediate national purpose and a dynamic growth strategy, the production behavior and performance of the big farmer across the road is more relevant. Approximately 800 miles away, Bir Babu too fits the description. Farmers like them operate a critical portion of the arable land in the country.

Ironically, and perhaps inadvertently, Mohinder places these large landowners, who lack for nothing, in the same category as the lowly Harijans, who possess little or nothing. And for the same reason. The two extremes of the rural hierarchy, who differ in respect of every factor and option, appear to suffer from a stubborn incapacity for efficient husbandry. Mohinder, a Sikh and a Jat, clearly sees himself as *different* from both—in yet another category, a category of cultivators who are generally very successful. They are successful, according to him, primarily because they are born to the "profession."

But what about the Green, or so-called Wheat Revolution? Has it not transformed everything? Glowing accounts are being written around the world, of how the new seeds have induced changes in the minds of peasants, in their attitudes and outlook, that are truly revolutionary. It is said that farmers who previously lacked enterprise and receptivity to new ideas have now become efficient, production- and profit-minded, with a "will for material progress typical of capitalism." Isn't all this true?

"Yes. This Green Revolution *was* here."

He speaks of it in the past tense. As if it were an episode on the shelf of history.

"It was our good luck that we got the new strains—the high-yielding varieties. Production went up because of them, and we made a big noise about it. But it was not that big. And it was not that lasting. It was not that lasting because, for one thing, we did not use enough fertilizer in the beginning. Not as much as was needed by the new varieties."

There was a spurt in yields for a while. "Then all of a sudden certain deficiencies and imbalances developed in the soil, for which we need some other elements. The scientists have been struggling with the problem. And now, unfortunately, fertilizer is not available. So, the speed of the Green Revolution has slowed down."

You cannot get fertilizers?

"I am bothered about the common man. Not people like me. Yeh, I am all right. I plan ahead of time. And I can always request the officers to help me out. They will locate supplies and give me the information—where to go and get it. But then I, one person, cannot solve the food problem." He nevertheless claims the major credit. "Whatever success we have shown here, in the Punjab, with this Green Revolution, it is only because of farmers like me."

Government planners and social scientists, especially economists, would readily endorse Mohinder's claim. They too associate farmers like him with the impressive initial spread and success of the Green Revolution—but with an important difference.

Most scholar-observers would look upon Mohinder, not as the cause, but as the product of a sound technology and strategy of development. To them he personifies a *new* phenomenon in Indian agriculture, of a peasant turned farmer—"conscious of his new role, investing and experimenting with new practices"—a type or class of cultivators that has allegedly emerged only since the introduction of the high-yielding varieties program.

The success of the strategy itself would be ascribed to high prices and profitability of "miraculous" yields from the "miracle" seeds, used in combination with water and fertilizers. Mohinder's personal success would be attributed to a high level of schooling, and, therefore, managerial ability; adequate size of landholding; and preferential access to scarce inputs, influence, and information. All the factors, in other words, which in theory prescribe the nature and limits of economic response of any farm operator anywhere. Mohinder's explanation that a man's traditional "profession" or value system transcends these factors and is generally responsible for the often striking variations in the quality and standard of cultivation—even among big farmers who are equally well endowed—would be considered archaic, reactionary, and inadmissable for discussion, analysis, or action in any policy and planning forum in the country.

For policy and other considerations, in the somewhat imprecise jargon popularized by the Green Revolution, Mohinder would be described variously as a "kulak," "capitalist," or "gentleman farmer." Mohinder resents the labels and blames them on the traditional image of the farmer, the stereotype that most upper-class urban Indians carry in their minds.

He mimics "those city people sitting in air-conditioned offices. They will say, 'You see this man. He is wearing a necktie, a shirt, and a coat! Therefore, he is not a farmer. He must be a big landlord.'" That would make him a "feudal" landowner, nationally viewed as obsolete and as the most exploitive of the rural elite.

"This is the kind of image our people have. It is very sad. I work very hard. But I will be told, 'you are not a farmer. You are not a farmer'. We are not regarded as human beings. Recently, we received notice that the electricity for our tube-wells would be given only at night. Factories will get it during the day. We are fighting it. But do you think they would care to come and see what it is like to irrigate the fields in the dark, especially now, in this freezing cold weather?"

Due to power shortage, "some farmers have installed crude-oil engines on low-speed diesel fuel. But now diesel also is not available. That too is going for factory furnaces. So, they say, how are we to pump the water? And the time is gone that we can use bullocks and irrigate with the Persian wheel."

As if obsessed by the thought, and pointing to himself, he repeats: "You see, they cannot tolerate this jacket on a farmer. Farmer and good clothes? The *real* farmer wears a *langoti*. Not pants. Even if he wears a pyjama, he cannot be a genuine cultivator."

As a footnote, however, this caricature of the typical farmer, is not exclusively urban. With a twinkle in his eyes now, he recalls: "When we came here, I tell you, these neighboring villagers, they thought they would purchase our land, sooner or later, because they said, 'these *patloon wallahs,* they are not genuine farmers'. Secondly, we also had a tractor. And according to them, 'unless the bullock's feet are in your fields, you cannot grow a good crop'. So they said: 'They have got this tractor. They will therefore fail very soon, and we will purchase the land'. But after two or three years, when they saw the farm again, they were afraid. They were afraid that now *we* would purchase their lands."

What do you mean, you had a tractor when you came here? When did you get rid of your bullocks?

"Since we came here, we have never kept any bullocks . . . ."

When did you buy the tractor?

"In 1951. We started here with a tractor and diesel engine, because my father felt that we could not succeed without a tractor. And to us also, it was a big temptation—to have machinery. To drive a tractor. We did all the operations by tractor or hired labor."

You started here in 1951? But where did you come from? Were you refugees? So far, there had been no hint of it, and I had forgotten even to ask.

"Yes. We came from the district of Multan. Just to give you a brief story of my family. We came after partition. We were allotted this land in 1951, in exchange for the land that we had left behind in Pakistan."

Was your father a full-time farmer?

"Yes. My father was a farmer—he was a full-time farmer. That was his profession. At the time, my older brother also was here. We were both working. I was a student then."

You were studying and working on the farm at the same time?

"Oh, yes. We were working on the farm as well as going to college. I did Masters in economics. My younger brother, who is now in the States, he was in the engineering college. So, during the day we went to college. At night we drove the tractor and helped father with the work. I took charge only after 1965. But my father was still looking after the accounts and marketing. My responsibility was production. To produce, that was my job."

Incidentally, where did you acquire your American accent from?

"It is just an affectation," he replies, laughing. "I was under an exchange program—went to the United States in 1966. I was in Montana and Illinois. I stayed with farm families. In Montana, I saw their wheat cultivation, which is not as good as we have here. But in Illinois, the corn cultivation! Unbelievable yields they get—and that without irrigation. So I learned many things from there. I also saw their mechanization."

It partly explained Mohinder's enthusiasm for machinery, I thought. But why did your father think that the tractor was important? There were very few tractors in those days, in 1951.

"Because, as I told you earlier, with bullocks there are so many limitations. Almost half the land goes for growing fodder. That is what my father was preaching to these people— that small farmers should not farm with bullocks. If I have five acres, and I keep bullocks, two acres will be allotted for fodder. So only three acres are left to me. What will I do with three acres? So my father said that only big farmers can afford to maintain bullocks. Not small farmers.

"And then you see, we had to study at the same time. With bullocks, you have to work the whole day. With the tractor, when we came home in the evening, in two hours we could cultivate all the land, or do whatever else was required . . . ."

How much land did your family have in Multan?

"In Multan, my father owned 35 acres. Here we were given 25 acres. So in 1951, my father had that much land here—yes, 25 acres. That was how much land we had. But we took more land on rent. So we were actually cultivating about 60 to 70 acres.

"But when we came here in 1951," he recalls with a faraway look, "there was no house. *Nothing.* There was only one big tree. And no irrigation. This land was all unirrigated. What we did, the *first* thing we did, because my father was a good farmer, the first thing he said, 'Okay, don't sow any crop until you have leveled the land. Leveling of the soil, the land, is very, very important'. And that is what we did. My father spent a lot of money on just that, without growing any crop. We had come with empty hands. Then, by and by, we purchased more land. And now, it is 95 acres."

Is land available on rent? Are there many tenants here?

"Now? Very few. Most of the farmers here work themselves. These two villages, you see, they both started from scratch. Like us, they are refugees. We all came with empty hands. With hard labor and all that, we have built up. So this is . . . ."

It is the familiar saga of hundreds of thousands of farm families who were forced to leave their homes, property— ripening crops standing in the fields—in the wake of independence and partition of the state and country. As recounted more vividly some fifteen years earlier, by another group of refugees of Mohinder's father's generation:

> We came in the clothes we were wearing. Our only luggage consisted of cooked food for ourselves and rations for the animals. Of all our animals we brought with us just the two bullocks yoked to the cart. We came from the districts of Multan, Montgomery and Lyallpur. We did the whole 200-mile journey in our bullock carts.
>
> When we arrived here, in October 1947, this village was in ruins. It was a Muslim village and it had been burnt and looted. Not a single house was intact. Only two of them were of brick, and of those only the naked walls were standing. Land had been cultivated but the crop had been cut. We found a little maize standing, which we harvested. There were 25 percolation wells, but 20 of them had no water.

The first thing *they* did, "once the lands had been allotted to us, was to install tubewells." Not because they were used to tubewells—"in Pakistan we had canals." But because, like Mohinder, they refused to irrigate with the Persian wheel.

> We did not relish the idea of walking round and round with the Persian wheel. One of our men actually fell into the well while doing so. But then there was no electricity here.

That did not stall them.

. . . we formed a committee, collected 20 rupees per head, and applied for power. Niranjan Singh and Badan Singh were assigned to do the running around in the various offices, and finally, we obtained the necessary sanction. For tube-wells the government offered loans, not subsidies.

And then, in striking contrast to the cultivators (and Bir Babu) in Bihar, who repeatedly lost their crops because they expected the government to do everything, including what they could have very easily done themselves—:

We were so impatient that we did not allow the electricity department to install the line. As soon as the materials started arriving at the railway station we told the officials that there was no need for their hired labour doing "hay ho, hay ho." We would do the job ourselves. You see, we wanted to see the tube-wells working overnight, and you know how slowly the administration works.

So we fetched the materials in our own bullock carts. Over a stretch of three miles we dug the pits for the poles in just two days. In another three days we put the poles into position. One of us would tie one end of the rope round his waist and the other end to the pole and haul it into position. Then we did the wiring. We all worked, including the *Harijans* and the children. The whole village worked. It became a pleasure. Within less than a month all the work had been completed. The Government would have taken six months maybe. We made the tube-wells in the existing wells. Some of them needed extra boring. [Nair, *Blossoms in the Dust,* pp. 102–3]

Five

Prices and Perversity

Memories have dimmed, like streetlights after the dawn. A great many of the generation that bore the brunt of being uprooted are dead or retired. Only fifteen years ago, in the winter of 1958, I did not have to ask. The refugee was visible, eager to talk about the tragedy. And he spoke with emotion. With irony, often tinged with bitterness. But like Mohinder, with a cocky self-assurance. It was rather curious at the time. In his circumstances.

It was curious not only in a personal context of having lost literally everything and being forced to resettle in a strange environment on substantially less and inferior land. The confidence was the more striking in view of the singularly unpropitious climate for producers of foodgrains generally, and of wheat in particular, especially in the Punjab. Not only was the harvest of 1958 the poorest in five years, but throughout the decade farmers were confronted with:

> . . . declining incentives to farm output as the internal
> terms of trade moved against agricultural products, by in-
> adequate attention to supplies of agricultural inputs, and
> by neglect and poor administration of research, credit,
> extension, and other services necessary to an increase in agri-
> cultural productivity . . . . Under the impact of industrializa-
> tion programs oriented heavily toward import replacement,
> prices of farm inputs and of consumer goods used by the agri-
> cultural population rose, while the prices of foodgrains

and of some other farm outputs were held down by government action . . . . surplus wheat and rice in areas producing
surpluses were purchased by government at prices below the
market for sale in deficit areas . . . . Fertilizer prices . . . were
substantially higher than world market prices during the
whole period . . . . It is more than a surmise that the ready
availability of agricultural surpluses from the United States
had something to do with maintaining cereal prices at a low
level.[1]

India signed the first of a series of agreements under Title I
of the Public Law 480 in August 1956. Wheat was practically
the only cereal to be imported from the United States under
the arrangement—16.6 million metric tons in six years.

The imports represented a high proportion of the wheat produced within the country—in foul weather and fair. In the
poor crop year of 1958, for example, imports amounted to over
one-third of domestic production. And almost one-half two
years later, when there was a bumper wheat harvest—the best
since 1947. During 1960–64, moreover, 3½ million tons or
more of imported grain were released every year for public
consumption—even in 1961 and 1962, when food production
hit peak levels of over 82 million tons. This had two results,
observes K. N. Raj. First, not enough was left in stock for the
upcoming lean year.

> Second—and this has more significance from a long-run
> point of view—the large-scale releases of imported food-
> grains in the years of bumper harvests kept their prices at a
> low level relatively to the prices of manufactured products
> and created the impression that the Government had no
> interest in maintaining a structure of relative prices which
> would give incentive (or at least not create disincentive) for
> raising foodgrain production . . . . Raising productivity of
> land requires not only more inputs like labor, water and fer-
> tilizer but incentive to make these imputs worthwhile to
> agricultural producers.[2]

Not until late 1964 was the government persuaded to take
formal action to guarantee minimum prices for the major food
and commercial crops on a regular basis. And then, after the
event. In spite of continuing and increasingly larger flow of
imports, for example, the index number of prices of wheat had

shot up from 90 in 1962–63 to 146 in December 1964—an increase of over 60 percent.

For close to fifteen years, the government had been trying to accelerate agricultural growth in order to eliminate or substantially reduce the prevailing shortages. And the Planning Commission made progressively larger allocations for agriculture in each succeeding plan. It set production goals for every important crop "after careful consideration of basic requirements, market demands, supply potentials and investment programmes." But not only were the targets not achieved, but the principal commodity gaps between need and availability tended to increase. And most critically, for foodgrains. Even so, the change in pricing policy did not come easily. C. Subramaniam describes the situation and sentiments that he had to contend with when he became the Minister for Food and Agriculture in 1964:

> We had on hand a worsening inflationary spiral with demand for food going up as a consequence of increased incomes and population and the supplies growing but not fast enough. Even with an abundant crop, there was an imminent shortage of food . . . . While lip-service was paid to the concept of remunerative prices, in practice difficulties arose because of the cheap grain emphasis. In these circumstances, it was almost inevitable that my advocacy of higher incentive prices and a support price policy should have been received with less than enthusiasm by my colleagues in the Centre and the States. Many refused to see the obvious. I remember vividly how difficult it was to convince my colleagues . . . that in the long run, only a remunerative price could lead to self-sufficiency. It was fortunate for us that the compulsions of the crisis enabled the albeit reluctant acceptance of this policy.[3]

Finally, two new institutions were created in 1965—the Agricultural Prices Commission and the National Food Corporation. The latter functions as a public sector trading organization to handle internal procurement and distribution operations, as well as imports, on behalf of the government. The main function of the Prices Commission has been to make annual recommendations on minimum support prices for foodgrains and certain other crops, such as cotton, jute, and sugarcane. It also recommends the prices (and quantities) at which the government may purchase or procure foodgrains for public distribution through fair price shops and rationing. Among other things, the Commission was enjoined to keep in view "the need to provide incentive to the producer for adopting improved technology and for maximising production."

Ironically, just as the Prices Commission was established, the urgency or even relevance of minimum support prices was nullified by two droughts of unusual severity—in 1965, and again in 1966. Inevitably, the immediate concern of the Commission and the government became one of keeping a lid on prices rather than providing a floor. To do so, and to relieve the scarcity and near-famine conditions in several areas, a record 26.5 million tons of foodgrains were imported within three years.

By a more fortuitous coincidence, however, new fertilizer-responsive high-yielding seeds became available at the same time. Launched in 1966–67, the High Yielding Varieties (HYV) Program consisted of an exceedingly profitable package of factor inputs. The key components of the package were the dwarf varieties of (Mexican) wheat and (IRRI) rice, chemical fertilizers, irrigation, and pesticides. A fundamental claim for the strategy was its "emphasis on science and technology."

Apparently, the new technology triggered an almost instantaneous change in farmers' production attitudes and responses—"a dramatic break from their erstwhile behavior." Whereas the behavioral changes were reflected in myriads of everyday allocative decisions regarding the nature and quality of inputs and effort of each cultivator, the aggregate of these separate individual choices set the pace and pattern for a countrywide transformation of agriculture. Collectively, the changes in farm practices, production, and productivity were considered so remarkable that the phenomena earned the title of a *revolution*. According to Subramaniam, who was mainly responsible for evolving and introducing the program, the HYV strategy produced an altogether new environment. "To mention only one instance . . . minor irrigation which may have been only marginally profitable in traditional agriculture becomes very attractive in the new pattern . . . . This has led to a great deal of resurgence of investment in exploitation of groundwater resources in various parts of the country. Even the cropping pattern is changing making the land reproduce itself as it were."[4]

By 1968, the responsiveness of the allegedly backward tradition-bound farmers to the High Yielding Varieties Program was being acclaimed internationally as "one of the miracle-stories of modern development."

The new seeds spread with unexpected, almost unseemly haste. Twenty million acres were covered within two years or so. It could not have happened of course, but for the willing cooperation of the farmer—if he had not responded to the new economic incentives and opportunities. But then, as an eminent economist reiterated for the nth time: "farmers are not perverse in their economic behavior." If there has been perversity, it will be found in "the minds of many who shape economic policy . . . in what they behold in agriculture and in national economic plans that fail to provide economic incentives for farmers."[5]

Incentives are the crux of any scheme or strategy to improve productivity, according to T. W. Schultz, because in modern and traditional agricultures alike, farmers will make the requisite investment to produce more only if it is persuasively profitable to do so, with due allowance for risk and uncertainty. The rate of acceptance of a new practice or factor of production therefore depends upon, and is proportional to, its profitability—that is, the price and yield.[6]

Hailed as original and iconoclastic, the Schultzian formula had an irresistible appeal and ready acceptance in the weary, frustration-ridden centers of agricultural planning, research, and technical assistance. The underlying approach, assumptions, and especially the concept of "efficient but poor," became the philosophical basis of a new economic dogma, popular rhetoric, and national policy. Its principles were incorporated in the High Yielding Varieties strategy and received credit for sparking an unique agricultural revolution in several Third World countries.

Schultz's thesis also restored primacy of the classical view and concept of human nature in agriculture specifically. For like Adam Smith, who believed that "there was a Scotchman inside every man," the professor at Chicago visualized the Midwestern corn farmer inside every peasant. Whether the poor Indians in Guatemala or the highlands of Peru, or Indian peasants in the paddies and wheat fields of India, their economic behavior, affirmed Schultz, is no different from that of "the renowned farmers of Iowa."

In other words, if agriculture stagnates, it is not because "farmers, especially in poor countries, are loafers who prefer leisure to doing extra work to increase production." If they appear to loaf, it is only because the marginal return to additional work is too low. Nor would they gain significantly if they reallocated the production factors at their disposal, since they "are not capable of producing more under existing circumstances." Therefore, the factors need to be changed. Not farmers.

It follows then, that the farmers who produced massive deficits in foodgrains during the cheap food era of planned development in India, by not investing more in land and inputs and refusing to work harder, were acting in a *rational,* exemplary fashion. Except for Mohinder's family and father—Nanak Singh. By the same logic and criteria of economic rationality, Nanak Singh's behavior is puzzling, if not outright perverse.

Driven from his 35 acres of canal-irrigated land in Multan, Nanak Singh, middle-aged, with a wife and four sons, received 25 arid acres in compensation in Ludhiana in 1951. He was eligible for modest loans only for repairs of house and well, and for the purchase of bullocks, fodder, and a few simple implements.

At the time, crippled by the loss of sixteen districts covering 62 percent of the undivided state's area, 70 percent of its richest canal-irrigated lands, 69.9 percent of its income, and swamped by over four million destitute refugees, the administration and economy of the Punjab (India) were in a fairly chaotic condition, in the process of reorganization. The federal government in New Delhi also was preoccupied with its new identity, status, role, and responsibilities as a sovereign state. The first Constitution of the Republic came into force on January 26, 1950. In March of the same year, a Planning Commission was established. Not until 1953 was the decision made to create a National Extension Service in combination with a Community Development Program. The block, where Mohinder's farm is situated, was not sanctioned until 1954. Not until 1961 did Ludhiana become an IADP district. The Punjab Agricultural University that played a dynamic role in research and extension during the early years of the Green Revolution was not established until October 1962. Local *Panchayati Raj* institutions were still a decade away.

And so in 1951, aside from the market price signals, farmers in Ludhiana had to rely almost entirely on their own unaided whim, wisdom, experience, and initiative in making investment and production choices. On the other hand, national policy with regard to large imports and low prices for producers of foodgrains did not wait for the PL 480 supplies to become available in 1956. In the preceding five years (1951–55), over twelve million tons of cereals were purchased abroad and paid for in scarce foreign exchange.

Indeed, 1951 and 1952, when Nanak Singh was just starting to rehabilitate himself, were very difficult years. There was widespread failure of the *kharif* crop in the first year and of the *rabi* crop in the second year. Production of cereals declined. But strangely, so did their prices.

The end of 1951, in fact, marked the turning point for foodgrains—the transition from a sellers' to a buyers' market. Due to increased imports, a general recession and break in commodity markets in 1952, prospects of a good crop in the following year, and a variety of public policy measures, wholesale prices of cereals fell "so far and so fast" that even the government was alarmed and announced a general policy of price support. It failed to boost the market, however. By March-June 1955, prices of wheat and rice had declined by more than 30 percent (1952–53 = 100). But they were higher than the support prices fixed by the government. Consequently, except for the normal seasonal fluctuations, farm prices continued to fall sharply until mid 1955, when the government started negotiating for more imports under Public Law 480.

Such were the circumstances and prospects in agriculture, when with borrowed funds Nanak Singh decided to invest in a tractor instead of a pair of bullocks. Of foreign manufacture, tractors were costly and rare on farms in 1951. There were only 8,635 in the whole country. Similarly, although minor irrigation was supposed to be "only marginally profitable in traditional agriculture," Nanak Singh invested in a tubewell instead of the Persian wheel. There were fourteen tubewells in the district in 1951. And he leveled the land before planting the first crop, an investment Bir Babu did not consider worthwhile even in 1974.

Throughout the decade moreover, the relative price of wheat—the major crop in Ludhiana and the Punjab—was the *lowest* compared to other cereals as well as to all other commodities. And in 1962–63, it was lower than in 1951–52. A farm management study of two districts in the state during 1954–57 shows a net loss of $9.87 per farm as a whole (crop production only).

Instead of going broke, however, Nanak Singh substantially expanded his farm operation, first by leasing more land and later by purchase. He built a new house. It was modest, but made of brick, nevertheless. And, he provided college educations for his sons. Even under more stable conditions, then and now, farm boys rarely finish elementary school.

All this, Nanak Singh did *prior* to the lush days of the Green Revolution—in a period of declining prices for wheat and other agricultural products, negative returns to farm management and investment, and a traditional low-yield crop technology. How can it be defended or explained?

The critic will argue that there always are, everywhere, exceptional individuals like Nanak Singh, who appear to be endowed with special entrepreneurial talents and propensities. Education, moreover, provides additional skills and enhances the capacity to make the right choices between complex alternatives. It has a positive effect on economic performance of any kind. A survey of Indian agriculture in 1960–61, for example, showed that the level of productivity was related to schooling. Even with traditional varieties, the better-educated farmers used larger amounts of chemical fertilizers and obtained higher yields than the less educated and illiterate cultivators. Clearly, Nanak Singh was no ordinary illiterate peasant, any more than his son Mohinder is. Aside from being literate, moreover, Nanak Singh had migrated from a higher income region and farm that he had been forced to abandon for reasons beyond his ken and control. That in itself would provide a drive and motivation to succeed against all odds that farmers like Bir Babu, captive in a prolonged stationary state, could not be expected to display, even if they are educated. Often, the very consequence of such disruption becomes an opportunity, and fortunately, Nanak Singh had the capacity to respond efficiently, if not entirely rationally, in an economist's scale.

Six

"I Wanted a Tractor"

If Nanak Singh, however, chose to invest in and modernize his farm some fifteen years before the first strains of the Mexican dwarf wheat—PV-18 and Kalyan Sona 227—were released for general cultivation in 1966 and 1967, respectively, because he was literate and a refugee, how does one explain the behavior of yet another Ludhiana farmer by the name of Jaswant Singh?

About the same age as Mohinder, he too has three brothers. Father is dead, but an uncle (father's brother) is living. All brothers work full time on the farm with Jaswant in charge of production. They jointly own and cultivate one hundred acres in the village of Khera Bet.

Jaswant first cultivated Kalyan commercially in 1968, as soon as enough seed was available. His yields have been as good as of Mohinder Singh, but, as in the rest of the state, on the decline.[1] "The seed that used to give twenty quintals to an acre gives only fifteen or less now. Yet, I apply three quintals of fertilizer and add compost later. When we got the new seed, this land did not need much fertilizer. We used to say that 50 kilos is enough; more than enough. But from the third year on, the soil began to take more and more fertilizer and the net income started to decline." Aside from wheat, for the first time last season, Jaswant sold paddy—a new crop in the Punjab—worth one hundred thousand rupees. He also grows maize.

Like Mohinder, Jaswant too has mechanized. He owns a

combine harvester, two tractors with plow, harrow, cultivator, seed drill, corn planter, trailer, and so on. And a jeep. He has three tubewells for irrigation. "This soil is sandy. It takes more water." The only animals on the farm are five buffaloes, for milk. "It is all consumed within the family." Not sold.

Unlike Mohinder's family, however, Jaswant did not migrate from Pakistan. He was born and raised in Pamali, a small village about ten miles from Ludhiana city. Furthermore, he is illiterate, with no skills for any occupation other than agriculture. "Ever since I can remember, we had only one job—to work on the land. That is why none of us could get an education."

Unlettered and untraveled, Jaswant is, in fact, far more typical than Mohinder of the great majority of the rural population, the small cultivators. He could never pass for a "gentleman farmer." Tall, lissom, broad shouldered with handsome, sensitive features, he is attired in an open-collared shirt, sweater, and a turban loosely tied. The collar and cuffs are frayed and the down-at-heel shoes unpolished. Broken fingernails. Unlike his counterparts in Purnea/Bihar, he wears pants instead of a *dhoti*. But so does almost everyone else in Ludhiana, except the elderly, who feel more comfortable in a *tehmat*. Pants no longer symbolize social class or urbanity. He speaks only rustic Punjabi.

There are other differences between Mohinder and him. For example, Jaswant too has built a new house since 1964. "It is on the main road, on the right side as you enter the village. It is a *pucca* house with big heavy doors—*pucca* house." But unlike Mohinder's residence, it is of traditional design—single-storied, with a paved courtyard and rooms along the side. The only "modern" features, and they are not uncommon in these parts, are electric lights and fan. The furniture consists of a few rough-hewn wooden tables and chairs, and string *charpoys* that serve for both seating and sleeping.

Jaswant's management techniques are as rustic as his lifestyle. He is blissfully vague about his costs and returns because he keeps no accounts. Nor does he have an accountant. "The accountant will cheat me." He cannot say how much it cost to build the house. "Who knows? It has been built in bits and pieces. Some this year; some next year. We did not make it all at once." The daily household expenditure also is "an open account. Don't have the time to write it down. We all live and eat together. It is a large family and expenses are heavy. I have three children. One brother has four, one five, and one three. Yes, they are going to school."

Similarly, with regard to farm expenses. "All I know is that whatever the income, it is spent as soon as the crop is harvested. It comes from the soil, and returns to the soil." He is convinced moreover, that even educated farmers do not know their *real* costs and returns. "A *zamindar* does not count or calculate. If he stops to calculate, he becomes discouraged, frustrated. I sold paddy worth one hundred thousand rupees. It sounds like a lot of money. Had I saved half or even one-tenth of it, I would have been satisfied. But I didn't. Saving means that there should be a cash balance in the bank at the end of the year. We work very hard. True, we have a comfortable living, but no extravagant or wasteful habits. Yet, it all disappears."

Nevertheless, and despite the manifold differences in style and background, the *timing* and *nature* of Jaswant's production choices have been remarkably similar to those of Mohinder and Nanak Singh. Like them, he invested in more—as much— land, and in tubewells and tractors, in the years *preceding* the Green Revolution. Unlike them, however, he did so for no clear compelling reason, and from a much smaller land base. Together with two brothers, Jaswant's father owned *seven* acres, in all.

The seven acres belonging to Jaswant's family were sold in 1964. "The land in Pamali was expensive. This was cheap. So we sold that and bought this."

The land in Khera Bet was cheap because it lay in a *bet* or low-lying floodplain of the Sutlej—with swamps, sandbars, and many abandoned channels of the river marked by intense braiding. Much of the land was uncultivable and uninhabit- able until the construction of the Bhakra Dam in 1952 and the opening of the Nangel Hydel Channel and a network of irriga- tion canals two years later. Thereafter, most of the cultivable land was reclaimed, and a number of refugee farm families

were settled in the floodplain. Except for a narrow tract along
the river, the area is now practically free from floods.

Many of the new settlers on the *bet* land, however, did not
prove to be good farmers. And they sold the land at any price
they could get. Jaswant got his from two such allottees. Like
Nanak Singh, they had fled from West Pakistan, but failed to
produce good enough crops or profit.

"They were not making any money. Yes, they lived here.
But they were *Banias*, traders by caste. They did not understand
agriculture."

Jaswant is a Jat Sikh. Like Mohinder, he too is convinced that members of noncultivating communities are
incapable of good husbandry. "There are some very big landowners here, *lale*. I tell you, they have so much land. They got
it cheap. But they are rotten cultivators. This is what happens
when you give land to traders and shopkeepers. Agriculture is
not in their blood. They do not appreciate the value of land."

Jaswant concedes that conditions were not easy in the early
years. "That land you see there, we should have preserved one
killa (acre) in its original condition, as it used to be. On this *bet*
land, tractors would overturn. Many tractors have broken
down here. Wild boar and deer used to destroy the crops. Now
there is no jungle. It has all been cleared."

On his first visit, in fact, even Jaswant's intuitive response
was to turn back. And he did. "I was afraid that we would die
of hunger here, starve. But we had already sold most of our
land. After selling it, we set out in search of cheaper land
elsewhere. So I returned to Khera Bet. This time I consulted
the *patwari*. He showed me this property and advised me to
take it. That is how we came here. That was in 1964.

"Yes, the land had been reclaimed. It was yielding crops.
They were cultivating it. When I saw it, wheat was in the
ground. They planted only wheat. There was no arrangement
for irrigation. There were nineteen surface wells, but not one
of them was working. The land was not level, and no bunds
had been made. They said, 'why make them? They are not
necessary'. You see, they were producing only one crop in the
year. That too, rain-fed."

Jaswant purchased 40 acres at first—the rest, two years

later. "I paid one thousand rupees an acre. It was a very good
price at the time in this area. But this is good land; very good
land." He made the initial payment in cash—"from the money
we got for our land in Pamali, plus savings. Also, I sold the
tractor."

Tractor?

"Yes, tractor. I had a tractor in Pamali. I bought it in
1958."

He had purchased his first tractor in 1958.

"My family was vehemently opposed to the idea. 'You want
to ruin us', they said. But I still wanted it." They agreed only
because Jaswant threatened to leave and take up some other
work. "I would not work on the farm, I said. I also consulted
Mohinder, and he encouraged me. 'Tractor will not hurt you',
he said. 'You should get one. I will buy it from you if it does
not work, or if you suffer a loss'. No, I did not even know how
to drive a tractor. And I wasn't going to keep a driver. So I
worked with Mohinder Singh for about twenty days, and he
taught me to drive it. Mohinder also told me that 'if the
tractor breaks down, just leave it there and let me know. I will
fix it.' Many times when it wouldn't work, I left it in the field
and Mohinder came and repaired it. I drove that tractor alone,
myself . . . ."

I wanted a tractor. Well, just like that. I knew absolutely
nothing about tractors. Simply felt that I should have one.
Expenses go up, but the extra cost is compensated . . . .
With tractor, with machinery, farming becomes more attractive. I had seen other farmers using it, and *that* was a
factor. I decided to buy one also—secondhand; any old
tractor . . . .

That was in 1958. It was a bleak year in a bleak decade for
all grain farmers. And more so, in the Punjab.

The tractor was sold six years later to help pay for the land in
Khera Bet, "because we wanted a bigger holding. The family
was large and growing, and there was no land we could rent. It
wasn't available any more. Father used to take on lease fifteen
acres or so every year. That is how we managed to pull along.
But I did not want to continue like that. Also, I wanted a
tractor. And seven acres were too small . . . .

"After getting this land, however, I took a loan from the bank, and I purchased two new tractors. That is how I have two tractors now. You see, I couldn't go back to working with animals. I cannot and *will* not plow with bullocks again. But then with tractors, I must have sufficient land to cultivate."

Naturally, the expenditure on equipment and inputs increased greatly after the move to Khera Bet. And it accelerated further with the adoption of the high-yielding varieties— *"desi* wheat did not (and could not) take three quintals of fertilizer per acre." Nevertheless, it was the first tractor that Jaswant purchased in 1958, for no clear economic reason or gain—and *not* Kalyan, the new wheat variety that he adopted because it was profitable a decade later—that proved to be the catalyst that initiated the process for subsequent expansion and change.

Even the investment in land in a *bet* area, then a virtual wilderness compared to the fertile and intensely developed region around Pamali, was motivated primarily not by golden vistas of new opportunity, but because big farmers in the neighborhood discontinued their traditional practice of giving land to sharecroppers. And seven acres alone could not possibly support a four-wheel tractor. Since Jaswant refused to sacrifice the tractor, he had no option but to buy more land wherever he could find it for the price he could afford. Or quit farming.

The substantially larger size of the new landholding of course enabled Jaswant to purchase more and bigger machines. But the subsequent changes were essentially statistical, of scale rather than quality. The two new tractors, for example, merely replaced the older model. Combine harvester was a variation on the theme. And tubewells broke no tradition because the land in Pamali also was irrigated and double-cropped.

On the contrary, the *first* tractor replaced the immemorial and sacred bull—a fundamentally different principle of generating draft power. Aside from yielding psychic satisfaction, of status, speed, and comfort perhaps, the switch from animal to mechanical plowing alone had transformed the economic and philosophical foundations of the seven-acre farm in Pamali, *prior* to any change in seed, land size, or price structure.

It happened because, as explained by Mohinder, bullocks

require fodder for which a certain proportion of the acreage has to be reserved, even at the cost of food for the family. (Because there is not much pasture land in the Punjab, the fodder crops are raised on the farm. Normally, fertile irrigated land, approximately 0.2 acre per animal, is used for the purpose.) But the tractor needs fuel oil and, hence, cash before every plowing. It involves considerable modification of the traditional land use and cropping system. It also reduces operational flexibility, since, like the poor, animals will work on starvation rations, as no machine will. Consequently, instead of selling (or bartering) an indeterminate portion of his produce only when there was an exigency or surplus to spare, with the tractor, Jaswant was forced to produce a certain volume specifically for the market, to earn sufficient cash to pay for a fixed quantity of fuel, not to mention the spare parts, which again, no bullock requires. Not only did it severely narrow his choices, but, for the first time, prices—of crops and inputs—that used to be of peripheral interest, assumed vital importance.

A predominantly subsistence operation was thus converted into a commercial enterprise—a transition of momentous significance, without which the Green Revolution technology would have come only as a minor, if not wholly irrelevant, sequel.

Seven

Seven Acres and Two Plows

It would appear as if for Jaswant life began only in 1958, "when we got the tractor . . . ." Given his bias for machines, the developments that followed were logical, though by no means inevitable. Few of the farmers who bought a tractor, for instance, found it necessary to buy a combine harvester as well, as Jaswant did. Bir Babu did not. And even in the Punjab, there were less than 250 combines in 1971, against some 35,000 tractors and over one million plows.

It is still not clear, however, why Jaswant got a tractor in the first place, an arbitrary, high-risk innovation that was to transform most of everything—the quality of life, preferences, agricultural practices and mores, to which he was born. As described earlier, the economic climate for wheat producers in the state was as gloomy in 1958 as it was in 1951, when Nanak Singh made a similar choice. But in any case, to a normal peasant household with seven acres of land, the tractor can only have symbolized an improbable and irrelevant fantasy.

Jaswant does not speak of the days when he walked behind a bullock-drawn plow. Maybe he was too young and, therefore, does not remember. Maybe he does not want to remember, especially in the presence of a stranger. Fortunately, his uncle Gurmukh Singh has not forgotten. And he tells it, as it was.

"I had two brothers. I am 80 years old. I never married.

Never *did* marry," he repeats cheerfully with a broad, toothless smile.

In a dark blue *tehmat* and turban, Gurmukh Singh is very gray and wrinkled. But alert and bright, with a warm sense of humor. Contrary to conventional belief that the poor want more children because of their high utility and low survival rate, however, Gurmukh Singh sacrificed conjugal bliss "because how could we have brought up more children on seven acres? That is why I did not marry."

Not that infant mortality was not high in the district—over 193 per thousand births in the year of independence. Pamali itself was a tiny backward village unconnected with the outer world by rail or road. Even in 1961, it had only 144 households and one primary school—its solitary civic amenity. There was still no medic, dispensary or health center; no post office, safe drinking water supply, or electricity for domestic or agricultural use in Pamali. It could not have had less in Gurmukh Singh's time, half a century or more earlier.

> We had seven acres, two plows, four bullocks and one camel. We used to keep cows and buffaloes also—two to three buffaloes and five or six cows. Buffaloes provided milk for the family. No, we did not sell any milk. And the cows gave birth to calves, so we did not have to purchase any bullocks. [Echoes of Bir Babu]

"On the farm, we worked with our hands. Plowed the land ourselves. We did not engage any wage labor. Did all the work ourself. It was hard work. I also drove the bullock cart for hire, to transport grain and goods to the market in Ludhiana for other cultivators. I used to charge two rupees per cartload and bring in the earnings to supplement the income from the farm."

But could you support the family on that income? Did these boys have enough to eat? How did you manage?

"Yes, we had enough to eat. Had enough milk. Also, our expenses were less. There were no expenses. We never had tea, or sugar. Yogurt and buttermilk were our mainstay. In the morning my father would take a big glass of *lassi* with one thick *roti* before going to work in the fields. We drank a lot of *lassi*. No one knew about tea in those days. No liquor either.

We never took liquor except at a wedding or some such festive occasion."

What about clothing?

"We made our own. We would spin the yarn and weave it. We wore *khaddar*. That is what we used to wear. We made it at home."

What did you purchase in the market then? How did you spend your income?

"We? What did we spend on? Why, we never went to the bazaar. Only when there was a marriage in the family did we go shopping to Ludhiana." His eyes twinkle with amusement as he recalls. "Spend? Spend on a marriage? I tell you, for the marriage of Jaswant's mother, for that girl, we spent a total of two hundred rupees—just two hundred. Two hundred rupees and *desi ghee*. That is what we spent. It would be unthinkable now."

What would you spend now?

Jaswant answers. "Now it would cost fifteen thousand rupees to marry a son and twenty to twenty-five thousand for a girl. Not less. That would be the average."

It is a measure as good as any of the distance Jaswant has traveled . . . .

We may never know why Jaswant chose to abandon the virtuous rhythm of hard work and frugal living described by Gurmukh Singh. Mechanization of tillage did not improve the yield of the tall C306 variety—a progeny of Pusa wheat—and the maize they were cultivating at the time. Nor did it alter the intensity of cropping. Only the cost increased. Of more practical interest perhaps, is the fact that this family had saved, and enough apparently, to permit such a venturous investment in an alien technology.

Jaswant's explanation is that "the cost of cultivating *desi* wheat was so low that it was possible to save. That is how I could buy this land also from our own earnings. No one can do it now." On the contrary, whereas "production costs, of labor, inputs, just *everything,* have gone up tremendously in the last three years or so, the net income keeps getting less and less. Yes, I wear pants instead of a *tehmat.* And I ride in a jeep. Previously, at the most, it would have been a bicycle. But that also costs more. Nor can these expenses be reduced now, I feel, any more than the expenditures on fertilizers and fuel. No way. It has meant that there are no savings now."

Due to the cost-price squeeze, Jaswant wants to increase the size of the farm. "It should not be less than 200 acres. There is the question of capital. I do not have the money. But I could get a loan." He has been reluctant to purchase more land, however, because of the farm policies generally, and the ceiling legislation in particular. Jaswant's views on land reform are very similar to those of Mohinder Singh. He too believes that instead of restricting the acreage per household, government should impose a levy and mandatory standards of efficiency on production. "Every farmer should be required to produce a certain minimum from a given piece of land, and contribute a fixed quantity of grain to the government stock. *If he fails to do so, the land should be taken away from him.* But if the present ceiling is reduced further, indiscriminately, for all cultivators, production will go down . . . ."

Eight

In Bihar:
The Nonrevolutionary Revolution

Whatever the future of "professional" but seemingly "perverse" farmers like Jaswant and Mohinder in Indian agriculture, they did for a while make the Green Revolution in Ludhiana a legend, and in the Punjab, a unique success.

Similarly, Bir Babu's production behavior and low yields reflected an equally unimpressive performance of the average cultivator in Bihar. For despite the several land reforms, like Jaswant and Mohinder, Bir Babu represents the dominant class of *commercial* farmers in the district and state.

Traditionally rice is considered the principal grain crop in Bihar. According to state authorities, however, the impact of "miracle" rice on acreage and output has been disappointing and production "has almost stagnated." On the other hand, the same sources claim "a major breakthrough" and "phenomenal progress both in coverage and production of wheat." It is a rare event in Bihar for any crop plan to be fulfilled. The increase in area under the new wheat varieties, therefore, from 25,000 hectares in the base year of 1966–67 to 1,640,000 hectares in 1972–73, was virtually a miracle. Not only did it far exceed the planned target of 880,000 hectares for the last year of the Fourth Plan (1973–74), but it was more than three times the acreage under HYV paddy. (Of a total acreage of 4,715,000 hectares under rice cultivation in 1972–73, only 452,000 hectares were under the high yielding varieties.)

"High yielding dwarf wheat like Kalyan Sona and Sonalika had spread like wild fire. . . ."[1]

Between 1964–65 and 1970–71, in fact, the compound rate of growth of the area covered by HYV wheat was 11.6 percent per annum in Bihar compared to only 5.9 percent in Punjab (composite state of Punjab and Haryana). And by 1972–73, both the total wheat area and the portion under the high-yielding varieties in Bihar had outstripped that in Punjab in 1969–70 and 1970–71. But not so the total production. Nor productivity. (See table 8.1)

According to the Fifth Five Year Plan for Agriculture in Bihar (1974–79), moreover, the total production of wheat in 1978–79 would be four million metric tons on an area of three million hectares, of which two million hectares would be under the high-yielding strains. That would be close to half a million metric tons less than Punjab's output a decade earlier on about two-thirds of the acreage.[2] Similarly, the *anticipated* productivity of (all) wheat in Bihar in 1979, at 1330 kg per hectare, would be lower than that of Punjab almost a decade and a half earlier, in 1964–65 when *only* the indigenous varieties were under cultivation. (In 1964–65, the traditional varieties of wheat in the Punjab yielded an average of 1499 kg per hectare.)

The statistics encapsulate the approximate dimension of the difference, not in the rate of adoption of the new wheat, but in the average efficiency with which the majority of the cultivators in the same category of land size holding in the two states utilized, and are expected to utilize, identical factors of production—seed, pesticides, water, fertilizer, and, generally, the routine techniques of crop husbandry.

The differences stem from the quality and purity of the seed the farmers use; timeliness in sowing; control of weeds and pests; on-farm management of water, including the number of irrigations and drainage; and the quality, mix, and manner in which nutrients are applied to the soil. For example, the district of Ludhiana alone consumed twice as much fertilizer in 1973–74 as the entire state of Bihar did in the following year. And it showed—in the condition of the crop. The visual contrast, in fact, is probably a more valid measure than sta-

Table 8.1 Area and Production of Wheat in Bihar and Punjab (Reorganized) 1969–1973

	Bihar 1969–70	Punjab 1969–70	Bihar 1970–71	Punjab 1970–71	Bihar 1971–72	Punjab 1971–72	Bihar 1972–73	Punjab 1972–73
Total area under wheat cultivation (in thousands of hectares)	1145.0	2162.0	1315.6	2290.2	1397.4	2335.4	2509.1	2404.3
Area under HYV (in thousands of hectares)	437.0	1502.0	880.0	1589.0	1213.0	1695.0	1640.0	1884.0
Total Production (in thousands of metric tons)	1200.0	4800.0	1258.9	5145.0	2493.7	5618.0	3136.4	5368.0
Yield (kg/hect.)	1048	2220	957	2238	1785	2406	1250	2233

Source: Directorate of Economics and Statistics, Ministry of Agriculture and Irrigation.

tistics—of doubtful accuracy at best—of the efficiency gap in agricultural husbandry of the two regions. Thus:

It is the second week in January. The fields in Central Punjab are a lush dark green with a uniform stand of young healthy wheat. Patches of mustard and sugarcane. Practically, hardly, no fallows. Tubewells everywhere; an occasional Persian wheel.

A fortnight later, across the entire length of the rich Gangetic belt in Bihar—from Purnea in the northeast to Shahabad in the southwest—the crops are almost uniformly poor, mangy, undernourished, like the men, women and animals tending them. Wheat, gram, mustard, pulses. Plenty of fallows, stubbles of the last harvest still in the ground. The wheat is young for the season; sown late. Germination is uneven even on irrigated land; rarely in straight rows. All hues—from dark green, to pale, and yellowing. Around Arrah, in the heart of the IADP district, during two days of conducted tour, only three "good" fields of Mexican wheat. Two of them are demonstration plots on the property of "progressive" farmers. This is also the belt where most of the state's tractors and tubewells are concentrated. Yet, *every* tractor I see, is on the road near or inside a town, transporting goods and people, while bullocks plow the land. Paddy too is being threshed by bullocks. And winnowed by the wind, manually. As for lift irrigation, the age-old wooden *latha* continues to dominate the landscape. Rarely a tubewell; very rare . . . .

Instead of comparing the two states, however, perhaps individual districts would be more appropriate units for evaluating production trends. They are smaller and more homogeneous in terms of natural resources and environment. If we select Ludhiana in the Punjab, if for no other reason than the global notoriety it has now acquired, then Shahabad, rather than Purnea, would offer the closest parallel in Bihar.

The tenurial structure in Shahabad is similar to that in Purnea, with Rajput (and Brahman) landlords like Bir Babu owning, often, a whole village or more. Mostly flat and fertile, the land area in both districts is more than twice as large as Ludhiana. And precipitation is about double. Ludhiana is almost a desert by comparison. Also like Purnea, Shahabad is rich in surface water resources, with several streams and rivers. The most important of them, the Ganges and the Sone. Unlike Purnea, however, the district has been spared the ravages of a wayward Kosi. Kosi, too, has been contained since 1959, and no longer flows through Purnea. But whereas the latter district did not receive canal irrigation until 1965, Shahabad has a century-old canal system and the largest acreage under irrigation in Bihar. According to the Irrigation Commission of 1901–3:

> The idea of using the waters of the river Sone for irrigation originated about 50 years ago . . . . Sufficient progress had been made to allow of water being supplied through breaches in the banks of the Arrah Canal to the parched fields in the drought of 1873, and the canals were completed a few years after. They carry a maximum volume of 6,350 cusecs. About 80 per cent of the irrigation lies in the Shahabad district . . . .[3]

Ludhiana received its first canal irrigation in November 1882, with the opening of the Sirhind Canal. Both irrigation systems were remodeled and improved after 1950.

Like Ludhiana, moreover, Shahabad was one of the original seven districts selected for intensive agricultural development (IADP), also known as the Package Program, in 1960. Farmers of both districts, therefore, had the benefit of the same type of preferential and concentrated extension education and services for the same period. Purnea came under a modified version of the scheme, the Intensive Agricultural Area Program (IAAP), in 1965. Shahabad was the first district in Bihar to be chosen for intensive development, "because it is blessed with ideal conditions of agricultural production like fertile lands, irrigation and progressive aptitude of the farmers."[4]

The wheat tracts of Shahabad, in fact, were identified as typical of the best soils for the crop as early as 1886: " . . .the land is a rich alluvium annually enriched by the overflow of the Ganges; it is needless to say that no manure is required in this soil for the finest wheats, and that it is in this tract possible to grow as fine wheat as anywhere in India."[5]

Eight decades later, although Shahabad ranked twelfth

among the 80 major wheat-producing districts in the country, between 1966–69, along with Ludhiana, Shahabad achieved the most rapid progress among the IADP districts, "because of the high response obtained from the new HYV wheat when produced in combination with added irrigation and fertilizer."[6]

Finally, the area under wheat cultivation in Shahabad— 404,690 hectares in 1972–73—was the highest of any district in Bihar, and considerably higher than the 251,500 hectares in Ludhiana that same year. And so, whereas the new varieties of rice had only moderate success, despite the somber efforts of Japanese experts at the Indo-Japanese Agricultural Extension Center in Arrah since 1968, there was a "revolution" in wheat in Shahabad. According to a state evaluation report, "farmers in general have the craze for growing the latest varieties . . . ." The coverage of Mexican wheat increased from 11,672 hectares in 1966–67 to 231,291 hectares in 1971–72. Consequently, instead of farmers having "to procure grains to perform their festivals from the market," as they used to, Shahabad "has now become the granary of wheat for Bihar."[7]

Nevertheless, at 1493 kg per hectare, the yield of the high-yielding Mexican varieties in Shahabad in 1971–72 was less than the average in Ludhiana in the pre-Green Revolution and even the pre-IADP year of 1960–61. Furthermore, it was only about 200 kilograms more per hectare than that produced by Shahabad's own wheat cultivators in 1913–14. Almost sixty years ago, the yield of wheat in Shahabad district was 1283 kilograms per hectare.[8] Can a REVOLUTION be less revolutionary?

According to some economists, however, since the production and yield data can be manipulated in a variety of ways, a better test would be to ascertain whether the advent of the Green Revolution affected the attitudes and behavior of the farmer.

> An objective evidence in this respect can be provided by the change, if any, in his short and long-term investment decisions—in current inputs like fertilizers and land development through construction of tubewells and installation of irrigation pump-sets . . . . in absolute numbers, there

are millions who have demonstrated the change, whether it be in the use of HYV seeds and fertilizers, or digging wells and tubewells, and installing pump-sets on them, or purchase of tractors and power tillers. The upsurge in the use of these modern inputs since the advent of the new technology is phenomenal.[9]

Mere investment in modern inputs associated with the Green Revolution is thus regarded as proof of fundamental changes in the traditional attitudes and behavior of the cultivator. But as the data in Appendix 1 indicate, the difference in the scale and composition of investment between Punjab/Ludhiana and Bihar/Shahabad has been as significant and striking as the difference in the average efficiency with which the adopted inputs have been utilized by the majority of the farmers in the two states and districts.

Nine

In Punjab: Partition and Recovery

If Bihar is yet to be convulsed by an agricultural revolution, of green or any other hue, the green or wheat revolution in the Punjab is not the first, nor perhaps even the most revolutionary.

Whereas in colonial times, Punjab was normally a large exporter of wheat, the partitioned state of Punjab (excluding PEPSU, but including Haryana) was deficit in foodgrains at the time of independence. And its soils were less productive than in the regions inherited by Pakistan, because for over half a century most of the development resources of the composite province had been invested in massive irrigation projects in the northwestern districts. Of a total of 5.7 million hectares under canal irrigation in the old province, therefore, only 1.2 million hectares fell to the share of East Punjab in India.

The exchange of populations, moreover, was accompanied by extensive destruction of property, houses, and wells, and a near collapse of the state's administration and economy. Of the 2,701,929 displaced persons who fled West Pakistan, 1,600,321 were rural. Of the latter, like Nanak Singh, 617,401 were landowning farmers. In a number of districts, however, whereas the outgoing population had a high percentage of working peasants and agricultural laborers, many of those who replaced them had never worked on the land. In the allotment of agricultural land, no distinction was made between cultivating and noncultivating farmers. But no farmer received as much as he had owned in Pakistan because the Muslim evacuees abandoned much less acreage than the incoming refugees. A graded cut which hit the larger landowners the hardest was imposed. Altogether, "reduced holdings and poorer lands, a fall in the actual workers on the soil, insufficient irrigation facilities, slender capital resources and the rise of tenant interests, combine(d) to produce a picture of increasing economic pressure . . . ."[1]

Furthermore, even in the early years of critical shortages, both the procurement and free market prices of wheat were significantly lower in the Punjab than in Bihar, or even in the adjoining state of Uttar Pradesh. (See Appendix 2, tables 1, 2) Nevertheless, and in spite of the nightmarish dislocations of lives and the economy, in barely two and a half years, East Punjab was transformed from a deficit into a surplus state for foodgrains. Between 1947 and 1949, Punjab imported 219,000 tonnes of cereals. In 1950, in a single year, the same crippled state exported 203,000 tonnes of grain to feed populations in deficit states like Bihar which were untouched by the disturbances attending the country's partition. (See Appendix 2, table 4.) It could do so because the production of wheat had increased from 820,000 tonnes in 1947–48 to 1,196,000 tonnes in 1949–50. And of all cereals, from 1,549,000 tonnes to 2,126,000 tonnes in the same period. (See Appendix 2, table 5.) Thereafter, except for one bad year in 1951, never again would Punjab be short of food.

Water was about the only yield-increasing technology available to farmers at the time. The gross irrigated area increased from 1,609,828 hectares in 1947–48 to 1,780,137 hectares in 1949–50. Even that, however, was not the result of any major investment by the government in new irrigation projects. Completion of the towering Bhakra Dam was still several years away. Work on the canal system was not completed until 1954, though restricted supplies of water were made available for *kharif* crops only, from 1952. The dam was not finished until 1963. The census (1951) describes the irrigation works undertaken by the state government in this immediate post-partition period:

"1947–49 . . . . The floods of September, 1947 caused a

heavy damage to Madhopur headworks. Numerous breaches were caused in the marginal Bunds at Ferozepur headworks. An extensive damage was caused to the canals by the abnormally heavy rains as well as the heavy traffic of displaced persons over the canal banks. Necessary repairs were, however, effected to the banks and canals, the Madhopur headworks as well as the Ferozepur headworks."

Prices and price policies for foodgrains during the years that Nanak Singh was struggling to rebuild a new life in Ludhiana have been described briefly. Not only was the price of domestic wheat affected adversely by large imports and a cheap food policy, but throughout the 1950s and subsequently, it was lower in the Punjab than in most parts of the country. (See Appendix 2, tables 2, 3; Appendix 1, table 4).

Despite the low prices, however, not only did Punjab farmers extend wheat cultivation to new lands, but they utilized even the seasonal fallows for the purpose. Consequently, between 1952 and 1965, and *prior* to the varietal breakthrough, output of wheat in Ludhiana increased at a linear rate of 8.35 percent a year. Five districts did better. (See Appendix 2, table 6.) The growth rate of wheat production in the state as a whole was less, at 6.79 percent—achieved by an annual increase of 3.92 percent in area and 2.09 percent in yields. But it was the highest in the country, as was also the rate of growth in all-crop output—at 5.56 percent per annum in the same period. (See Appendix 2, table 7.) These data, moreover, pertain to the composite state of Punjab—inclusive of PEPSU and Haryana—before it was repartitioned for the last time in November 1966. Its geographical area then was larger and more heterogeneous than during the Green Revolution era.

There was considerable variation, however, in the pattern and pace of agricultural growth among the 17 districts of East Punjab, the rates ranging from 11.32 percent in Bhatinda to 1.14 percent in Gurdaspur. (See Appendix 2, table 8.) And again, although Ludhiana was among the six "very high" growth districts, it ranked sixth in increase of all-crop output, fifth in extension of cultivation, and sixth in productivity gains.

To achieve such impressive growth rates, district and statewise, a very large number of Punjabi farmers must have ventured, like Jaswant and Nanak Singh, to expand and modernize their farm operations in spite of declining prices for their produce, especially wheat; and the much-publicized fact that "there was little new, profitable technology for them to choose." Their behavior was reflected in a substantial increase, of almost equal magnitude, in fixed and working capital in the state's agriculture, during the decade and a half preceding the outbreak of the "revolution." More striking than the quantitative increase in investment, moreover, was the change in its composition, in new kinds of manufactured inputs and machinery. Items such as chemical fertilizers, tractors, tube-wells, electric pumps and oil engines, practically unknown in 1950, and generally unavailable except at inordinately high prices, with scarce or nonexistent credit and service institutions, had become commonplce in the Punjab by 1966. (See Appendix 2, tables 9, 10, 11.)

It could be argued, however, that during the first three Five Year Plans at least, the main trends of growth and investment in agriculture were similar throughout India. The variations were of degree; not kind. And most of them could be explained by economic, ecological, or institutional factors.

Nor was Punjab's performance the best in all respects. Between 1952 and 1965, for example, the all-crops productivity increased at a higher rate in Gujarat and Tamilnadu. In the latter state, the linear growth in output of the traditional varieties of rice was a vigorous 6.04 percent a year, accounted for by an increase of 3.19 percent in acreage and 2.19 percent in yields per acre.

Bihar also achieved an annual growth rate of 3.21 percent in all crops, and 3.28 percent in foodgrains in this period. Even the production of *desi* wheat increased at 2.35 percent a year. As for modern equipment, the state's farmers had purchased 2,132 tractors, 6,854 electric pumps, and 3,698 oil engines by 1966.

In respect of one crucial, though "traditional" yield-increasing input, namely, irrigation, however, the record of attitudes and practices of the farmers in Bihar, both before and since the Green Revolution, has been substantively different from that of Punjabi cultivators. Thus, unlike Punjab, the gross irrigated area in Bihar in 1968 was less than it was in 1950. And between 1943 and 1956, it had declined by over a million acres, not because of political disruption or economic collapse such as Punjab suffered in 1947, but "because the lack of proper care and attention made the old system largely ineffectual."

The "old system" consisted of rain and streamfed tanks and reservoirs formed by the construction of bunds across natural depressions, known as *aharas*. The latter were sometimes further supplied by ditches and small canals, called *pyens*, diverting water from the nearest drainage stream. According to the Report of the Indian Irrigation Commission of 1901–3:

> These works are essentially private—the property of the landowners . . . . the customary obligation to repair *pains* and *aharas* rests on the landowners . . . . It is true, however, that, owing to the sub-division of land, the landowner now rarely does his duty in keeping the *pain* silt-cleared and the *ahara* in repair . . . . these simple but valuable irrigation works are falling year by year into disrepair. There is no law to compel a person to carry out repairs, so they are not done . . . .[2]

The commission pointed out that expert or technical knowledge is scarcely required for the silt clearance of a tank or an irrigation channel. Nevertheless, the process of these irrigation works falling into disrepair continued after independence, and even after the abolition of *zamindari*. The new owner-cultivators displayed as little interest in their maintenance as their "feudal," and mostly absentee, landlords.

In the years preceding the Green Revolution, in fact, Bihar farmers made no capital investment in irrigation (see Appendix 2, table 12), relying primarily upon the deteriorating surface water sources, tanks and reservoirs, that were dependable only when the rains were good. And when the rains were good, they did not use much water. They did not irrigate the crops. Consequently, in 1965, a larger area than from all other sources combined—1,072,000 hectares—was still dependent on water from the traditional *aharas, pyens,* and tanks. And compared to over a million hectares in the Punjab, only 312,000 hectares were under well (including tubewell) irrigation in Bihar.

The big push for well irrigation in Bihar did not come until after the severe, though by no means the first, drought and famine of 1966–67, when the government undertook a massive program for drilling state tubewells in tracts with good groundwater resources. It also gave subsidies to farmers wishing to have their own, offering to sink the tubewells for them on their land. Nevertheless, even in 1971–72, the peak year of the Green Revolution, of a total of 2.4 million hectares under wet cultivation in Bihar, tubewells accounted for only 394,000 hectares, or less than half the area irrigated by the old non-perennial sources. In the Punjab (reorganized state), not only had all surface sources been abandoned by then, but tubewells alone were irrigating some 1.2 million hectares.[3] Over 99 percent of the tubewells represented private investment of the cultivators. Contrary to popular belief that Punjab is a favored canal-water paradise, moreover, wells of all description were irrigating a larger proportion—56.19 percent—of the irrigated land in the state in 1972.

The striking difference in private investment in minor irrigation works in the two states was reflected in the response of their farmers toward the water made available from costly public projects as well. By March 1972, for example, in terms of the created potential from major and medium irrigation works, Bihar was second in the country. Punjab was seventh. But whereas 97 percent of the potential irrigation was utilized in the Punjab, 39 percent of the irrigable area in Bihar remained unirrigated.

And so, although the Eastern Kosi canal was opened for irrigation in 1964, after seven years, whereas "the irrigation in *kharif* 1971 was 0.12 million hectares against 0.32 million hectares envisaged for the year . . . the present rabi irrigation is insignificant. There is, therefore, gross under-utilization *of the irrigation potential of this system, both in kharif and rabi.*"[4]

Furthermore, no appreciable headway had been made in the construction of field and drainage channels, because *"the farmers are reluctant to excavate field channels."* (Italics added.) Also because of farmer apathy, especially among the larger landowners, not much progress could be made with land leveling, without which irrigation would not be feasible in nearly 25 percent of the command area. Special staff and equipment were provided for the purpose, but "due to lack of adequate demand, the tractors are reported to have worked, on an average, for only 100 days in a year."[5]

Experience with the Gandak project in Bihar, begun in 1960, was similar to that of Kosi. Against a target of 55,000 hectares, only 18,000 hectares were actually irrigated in 1969–70. The Irrigation Commission of 1972, noted "with great concern that because attempts through the panchayats and lambardars to induce cultivators to construct channels have failed, the utilisation of water both in the Kosi and in the Gandak canal system actually dropped in 1969–70 compared with the previous years."[6]

Ten

Irrigation: For Survival or Profit

Kosi and Gandak are relatively new projects, and possibly the potential beneficiaries have not had time enough to learn, appreciate, and adjust to irrigated agriculture. But in the Sone basin in Bihar, with its century-old canal system as well, and unlike Punjab where *kharif* and *rabi* crops are irrigated almost equally, rice was raised on 71.2 percent of the total irrigated area against 20 percent of *rabi* wheat harvested in 1967–68. Furthermore, farmers would generally wait for the monsoon rains before applying for water from the canal. If the rains were adequate, there was little demand for canal water and the total area irrigated from the canal diminished considerably.[1]

Ironically, the nature of farmers' response to canal irrigation in the Sone valley, when it was first developed in the latter part of the nineteenth century, was practically identical with that of their descendents in the 1970s. Thus, "whereas in October 1875 the Government of India anticipated a yearly irrigated area of 1,043,680 acres, the average of the five years ending 1900–01 was only 463,181 acres, and the maximum ever attained was 555,156 acres, in 1896–97. [There was a severe drought in 1896–97.] The cultivated area commanded by the canals is 1,354,302 acres; so that about one-third of this is watered every year."[2]

Furthermore, according to the Irrigation Commission (1901–3), prior to the completion of the canals, it was anticipated that the chief demand for water would be for the *rabi* or cold weather irrigation, as had been found to be the case in the Punjab. "But it was soon found to be otherwise; and now nearly 70 percent of the whole irrigation is for the *kharif* or autumn crop which practically consists of rice . . . ."[3]

The rice crop too was not irrigated regularly. "It is, at first sight, astonishing," noted the commission, "that the *kharif* irrigation is not more extensive, for only once since the canals have been opened, has the water in the river not been sufficient . . . ." It is also astonishing that the explanation in the 1870s when the canals were first opened was the same as in 1970. It was because the traditional practice in Bihar "is to run the water off the rice fields (*nigar*) in September; and after this the crop must get at least one watering during a period of 14 days, called the *hathia*,—generally from the 26th September to the 10th of October. If there is a good rainfall during this period the rice will mature unaided by irrigation."[4] The *hathia* showers determine the fate of the rice harvest and the extent of irrigation in *kharif*. For 25 years (1945–70) the rainfall pattern showed the *hathia* to fail once in every four years in the north, and once in every three years in south Bihar. The demand for water from the canals fluctuated accordingly.

And *rabi* irrigation has always been negligible in Bihar because, as in most parts of north India, where rainfall is adequate, temperatures cold, and the rich alluvial soils are highly retentive of moisture, very few waterings are required for the crops to mature. Considerable reliance is placed on the winter rains to provide the extra water, and, generally, they do not fail. *Rabi* irrigation in Bihar, therefore, is even a lesser imperative than in *kharif,* although in both seasons, yields are significantly higher with irrigation than without.

By 1901, both the northwest and the northeastern regions had been opened up and linked by rail to external markets for agricultural produce. The districts irrigated by the Sone canals were served by the Moghul Sarai-Gaya Railway, as well as by navigation. Owing to "the original backwardness of the cultivators in resorting to it," moreover, not only were the water rates fixed at an exceedingly low level, but a special system of long leases was developed "in order to educate the cultivators as to the value of irrigation." Reportedly, rents and incomes of the landowners in the Sone command area also appreciated considerably. Nevertheless, aside from providing protection against famine, the canals were unproductive. By the end of 1901–2, the interest charges on the Sone works had exceeded the net revenue by over 21.5 million rupees, the average loss in the three preceding years amounting to more than half a million rupees annually.

The attitude of the Bihar farmers toward canal irrigation— to use it only to protect a crop rather than to increase production—determined also the pattern of their investment in and utilization of water from wells. Of the total cultivated area in 1900, only 0.5 percent was under well irrigation. And that too was concentrated mostly in the market gardening tracts around the large towns, such as Patna, where "numerous lever wells are dotted about, and in combination irrigate considerable plots of potatoes and other vegetable and garden produce."[5] They still did in 1970—miniscule vegetable plots cultivated by the Koeris.

The usual method of raising water, moreover, was by means of a weighted lever, worked manually. Consequently, the area irrigated by each well was exceedingly small. Five acres were regarded as a large area to be irrigated from a permanent well, and temporary wells sometimes watered as little as a twentieth of an acre. By comparison, in the Punjab, where 70 years ago also the bulk of irrigation was from wells, the area irrigated by each well averaged eleven acres, and in some districts, twice as much. But instead of the water being lifted in small pots by manual labor, teams of bullocks were used to haul a large leather bag or turn the Persian wheel.

The capacity of the wells in Bihar was lower, not because there was not sufficient groundwater, but because instead of penetrating the subsoil underlying the clay beds beneath the superficial layer of sandy soil, reliance was generally placed upon percolation from the upper strata only. The Irrigation Report pointed out that nowhere was it expensive to dig a well; nor did the water lie very deep. "In many parts it lies so close to the surface that temporary wells can be dug for very small sums." But temporary wells also were not popular; not even in years of acute scarcity. Attempts were made in north

Bihar, during the famine of 1896–97, to induce the people to dig such wells. But with poor success.[6]

It is difficult to say whether the primitive techniques of lifting water, which continue to prevail, determined the design and low capacity of the wells in Bihar, or vice versa. But in the all important rice districts also, despite the crop being subject almost routinely to recurrent failure of the monsoon, often widespread and severe, according to the Irrigation Commission of 1901, wells were little appreciated. The indifference may have been due to the fact that when the rain was insufficient for the maturing of the rice crop, wells did not provide enough water to save it over any large area. But they could have saved the *rabi,* and perhaps rice as well, that is, if there were more wells with more water, and if more efficient methods were used to bring it to the surface.

The immense value of wells in unirrigated as well as irrigated tracts dependent upon surface tanks with uncertain supplies is illustrated by the fact that in the famine years of 1896–97, whereas the area irrigated by tanks fell by nearly one and a half million acres in the British territories in India, that under well irrigation expanded by approximately two and a half million acres. Again, in 1899–1900, although the water supply had started to fail in many parts owing to a succession of dry years, well irrigation rose by more than a million acres.

The Irrigation Commission was convinced, therefore, that notwithstanding the apathy of the landowners, Bihar needed more wells. Among other measures, it recommended that systematic inquiry be conducted, particularly in the central and western plains, with a view to determine the places best suited to irrigation from permanent wells; the possibility of reaching for that purpose the spring supplies below the clay beds; and the feasibility for further extending the practice of irrigation from temporary wells, which had proved so valuable in times of drought in other areas. The commission suggested that an "intelligent" officer of the Agricultural Department be deputed to ascertain the obstacles to the extension of well irrigation in Bihar, because aside from *kharif,* "if it were found possible to teach the Bihar rayats to cultivate *rabi* with profit by means of permanent wells, and by means of temporary wells

to save or sow a *rabi* crop in a bad year, a valuable resource
would have been found . . . ."[7]

But the *rayats* in Bihar never did learn.

And so, through two world war booms, several recessions,
frequent droughts and famines, and despite a growing differential in productivity in favor of wet cultivation, the approach of Bihar *zamindars* to irrigation, *any irrigation*, of *rabi* or
kharif, remained basically one of *survival*. It was to use or
purchase water to save an endangered harvest rather than
to improve crop yields in years of adequate and timely
precipitation.

The typical Punjabi cultivator, on the contrary, appears to
have been born to the ethic of utilizing irrigation for production, protection, and *profit*. In most parts of the Punjab also,
especially in the districts that are now in India, crops will
mature without the aid of irrigation if the rain is normal and
evenly distributed. Nevertheless, and in spite of an extensive
and rapidly growing canal system financed by the government,
expansion of minor irrigation in the province was as phenomenal in the last century as it has been since 1947. (See
Appendix 3, table 1 a, b.) By 1900, wells were irrigating more
than 44 percent of the total area under irrigation from all
sources. "As a general rule," observed the commission, "the
construction of wells in the Punjab appears to be a simple
matter, which the people are quite able to carry out without
professional assistance." But that was not because it is simpler
or cheaper to dig wells in the Punjab than it is in Bihar. On
the contrary.

Similarly, and in conspicuous contrast to Bihar, the success
of canal irrigation in the Punjab is legend. In 1900–1901, the
direct return on capital outlay on Punjab's major irrigation
works was estimated at 11.2 percent, against an average of 1.9
percent on the Sone canals for the three years ending 1901–2.
(See Appendix 3, table 2.) In the next three decades, with land
revenue lagging, irrigation became the most important single
source of revenue for the province. More importantly, unlike
Bihar, the benefits of irrigation in Punjab, "are not con-
fined to the protection afforded against famine in years of

drought. *Even in years of normal rainfall the value of irrigation is appreciated as a means of increasing the profits of cultivation, and fairly constant demand for water may be anticipated.*"[8] (Italics added.)

Essentially, it was this difference in attitude of a very large number of cultivators in the two provinces, reflected in their investment in wells and sustained utilization of water from public canals in good years, and not, as is widely believed, the size of investment by the government in major irrigation works, that was responsible for possibly the *first* real transformation of Punjab's agriculture in modern times, for which there is no parallel yet in Bihar.

Between 1898 and 1914, for instance, wheat production in Punjab increased by about 60 percent. That of raw cotton, about four and a half times. (See Appendix 3, table 3.) Exports from the province of wheat alone increased from around 250,000 tons a year in the early 1890s, to an average of 561,000 tons in the five years ending 1922. It represented a remarkable growth in commercial spirit and commercialization of a predominantly subsistence farming. In the process, "some of the ugliest and dreariest country in the world" was turned into "one of the granaries of the world."

It is true that during 1898–1914, almost half of the gross investment by the Indian administration in irrigation was made in the Punjab. Of the major canal systems, the Lower Chenab, Lower Jhelum, Upper Chenab, and Lower Bari Doab were all completed in this period. But the colonial government's decision itself, to invest or not to invest in a particular region, was in considerable part influenced by the prospective response of the cultivators. The financial fate of a project depended upon it. For works in north Bihar, for example, the Irrigation Commission (1901–3) was loath to recommend a modest expenditure of Rs. 800,000, "as long as the people are unwilling to take or pay for the water except during periods of drought. . . . We can hardly, in the light of past experience . . . suppose that the work will be other than unproductive."[9]

Even in the Punjab, in spite of the phenomenal profits of irrigation works, in recommending grants-in-aid toward the construction of wells in the arid southeastern districts, "in places where the spring level is not too deep for them to be worked with some small margin of profit, but where the margin is so small, and the difficulties and cost of construction so great, that private enterprise cannot be expected to come forward without such assistance," the Irrigation Commission reiterated that

> . . . regard must be paid to the character or class of the cultivator; to the facilities that have been held out to him in the past; and to the question whether any increase in these facilities will materially stimulate the construction of such works. The success of well cultivation, in tracts where the profits must in any case be small, depends so much on good husbandry or the capacity and industry of the cultivator, that this must always be a determining factor when State aid is proposed for private protective works.[10]

Eleven

Caste, Class, and Character

*. . . regard must be paid to the
character or class of the cultivator.*

Earlier in this and the past century, British economists and administrators were generally convinced of the central role of "character" in determining the direction and rate of economic progress everywhere, in Asia and Europe. In England, Alfred Marshall noted that "the first great undertaking, that of drainage on a large scale, was carried out for her by Dutchmen; the first English iron cannons had been cast in Sussex by a Frenchman; and lessons from French and Italians, Dutch and Flemings, Germans and Swedes had been required to equip Englishmen as workers in cloth and silk, pottery and paper, as miners and metallurgists."[1] In India, "character" was perceived as distinctive attitudes and behavior unique to particular castes and tribes—a legacy of undetermined origin and antiquity which transcended religious and regional boundaries.

In the Punjab, for example, the Jat may be a Hindu, Mohammadan, or Sikh, and "to some extent his characteristics vary accordingly . . . . All three, however, have a tenacity of character and a skill in farming which make them the best cultivators in India."

The Rajput, on the other hand, "although unusually intelligent and progressive," was considered to be "the worst cultivator." If of pure descent, he is forbidden to touch the plow. If not bound by the rule, "where the Jat ploughs deep he will only scratch the surface of the soil. His hedging and weeding are equally superficial."

Similarly, among the trading castes, the Bania, "half shopkeeper, half lender and wholly usurer," was seen as timid but so subtle and skillful that he "could give lessons to the most cunning Jews." Or the Aurora, also known as Kirar. "His greed for grain," wrote Thorburn in 1885, "the shameless effrontery with which he adds 50 percent to a debt, calls the total principal, causes his debtor to execute a bond for that principal with interest at 36 percent per annum more. . . . Such hard business qualities make him feared, hated, and despised by the agricultural classes."[2]

During the latter half of the nineteenth century, therefore, when in lieu of debt, land in the Punjab began to be transferred with "appalling rapidity" from its old owners to men "always of a different caste . . . inferior in physique and inferior in moral calibre to the men whom they supplanted," the administration became seriously concerned for the fate of the agriculturists and agriculture. It was to be expected, and so it happened, that "with a few brilliant exceptions, the new owner, drawn from the professional and trading classes, does not cultivate the land himself; he does not invest any capital in improving it; or devote his undoubted intelligence to the promotion of agriculture, but contents himself with obtaining the best rent he can."[3]

The problem of land transfers itself was new, because prior to British annexation of Punjab (1849), alienation of ancestral property was restricted by custom and tribal law administered by village and caste *panchayats*. "Strangers were jealously excluded from cultivating communities; and what is known as the right of pre-emption was closely watched." In effect, the individual cultivator possessed no rights in the land that he could alienate.

The very first settlements in the 1850s, however, produced tens of thousands of owner-cultivators with new legal rights of sale, mortgage, and hereditary transfer of land. That along with new laws, civil court procedures, and lower but more rigorously collected taxes than had been customary under the Sikhs resulted in a ruinous expansion of peasant indebtedness. For the first time, land that had been practically unsaleable became a valuable asset and an attractive investment. Also for the first time, it became easy for the urban and professional classes with capital to acquire land.

Consequently, "transfers of land were proceeding in all districts in an increasing ratio, and in many with dangerous rapidity." Between 1866 and 1874, an average of 231,000 acres were mortgaged or sold every year. By 1878, 7 percent of the province had been pledged. To stem the tide, not only did the colonial government decide to prohibit all sales of farm land in execution of a money decree, but after several years of debate and soul searching, and in violation of the ruling principle of the time, of nonintervention in the "natural economic process," it resorted to a discriminatory "class legislation" to protect the "agriculturist"—peasant and landlord alike—from further encroachment by the "nonagricultural" castes and interest groups.

The Punjab Alienation of Land Act was enacted and came into force on June 8, 1901. Thereafter, members of "notified agricultural tribes" were forbidden to sell their land to anyone outside their own tribe or community. Land could be mortgaged to "nonagriculturists" only temporarily, with a proviso for automatic redemption. Beginning with the first notifications in 1901, the local government published lists of "agricultural tribes" in each district which would qualify for the purposes of the act.

The Punjab Alienation of Land Bill evoked a vehement and virtually unanimous opposition from the Indian National Congress Party and the educated "nationalist" opinion and press. It was variously condemned as a "retrograde measure" calculated to "decrease the credit of agriculturists and landholders"; a political conspiracy to "divide and rule"; and an unjustified interference in the rights of private property.

Later Indian commentators, including economists, have generally ignored or criticized the legislation on the ground that it failed to achieve its main objectives. Since it did not apply with retroactive effect, for instance, the "nonagriculturists" who had acquired land prior to 1900 were not dispossessed. There were the inevitable evasions, corruption, and manipulation of the law. Above all, charge the critics, the act failed to eliminate or even to alleviate significantly the poverty and indebtedness of the peasant. On the contrary, agricultural debt and the area under tenancy increased substantially. Private transactions of mortgage and sale of land also persisted on a large scale, the farmers now borrowing from members of their own caste or tribe. A new class of "agriculturist" moneylenders emerged, the most prominent among them, "the Sikh Jat in the central Punjab, who has some of the canny business flair of the lowland Scot." The "agriculturist" landlord cum *sahukar,* moreover, took full advantage of the lawful opportunity "to add to his acres at the expense of the peasantry." And often he was even more harsh and exacting than the Bania or Kirar, for unlike them he was genuinely interested in possessing the mortgaged land instead of merely retaining control over its produce.

All of which is true. But irrelevant. For regardless of deeper, possibly political, motives underlying its enactment, the Land Alienation Bill was not meant to deal with the larger problems of rural poverty, indebtedness, and credit. Other measures, such as the Co-operative Societies Act of 1904, were adopted for the purpose. Nor did the fact and consequences of farmers taking to moneylending because of the restraints imposed on borrowing from other communities disturb the imperial administration, because again, this particular act was not intended to protect the peasant or tenant from the landlord; or any of them from incurring debts and selling or acquiring each other's property. It was never meant to stop *all* transactions in land. Only to restrict them among certain communities because, "in a country where the means of livelihood are divided into hereditary pursuits, there is more economic objection to land passing into the possession of non-agriculturists than there is to its accumulation in the hands of hereditary agriculturists."[4]

In its stated goal of retaining land in the possession of "agriculturists," who, according to contemporaries like Mohinder Singh also, are good farmers mainly because "agriculture is in our blood, our inheritance—the profession we are born to," the Alienation Act was largely successful.[5]

The principle of restricting ownership of agricultural land (or any property) on the basis of caste, profession, race, or

religion, was totally rejected after independence and pro-
scribed by the constitution. It was now assumed that any and
everyone, regardless of caste and class origins, could be a
proficient farmer, provided he is not hindered by ignorance,
malnutrition, or fiscal, technological, and institutional constraints over which he has no control. To "liberate" the vast
mass of cultivators from such constraints, and thereby "un-
leash" their inherent initiative and enterprise, became the central goal of national farm policy.

And so, for purposes of official record, development and
investment strategies, the peasants and landlords were, hence-
forth, equated, as if they were without history and without
tradition—a homogenous group differentiated only on the bases
of opportunity, tenure, and the size, quality, and location of
the land. A virtual moratorium was imposed on economic
analysis, or even recognition, of the most obvious differences in
values, attitudes, and behavior of the various castes and
communities.

The most important consequence of the new approach and
policy, however, was that the designated "agricultural tribes"
in the Punjab (and Haryana)—such as the Jats—were deprived of protection under the Alienation of Land Act of
1900. But in the permanently settled states, such as Bihar,
even after the abolition of *zamindari, zamindars* like Bir Babu
were reaffirmed in possession of most and generally the best land
in the rural areas.

As in the Punjab in the nineteenth century, and for identical
reasons, in the early years of the East Indian Company rule
in Bihar and other territories also, large areas of agricultural land had passed into the hands of urban traders and
moneylenders—*mahajans* and *sahukars.* Unlike Punjab, however, not only was the process allowed to continue unchecked,
but on the basis of a permanent settlement in 1793, this "new
class" of owners, who were not of the "old nobility" and had no
hereditary connection with the land, were confirmed as landlords. Consequently: "Very few estates of our times can trace
back their origin to a date prior to the advent of the British in

India. . . . the forefathers of many a zamindar of our times were either village headmen, or farmers of revenue, or sureties of defaulting zamindars, dishonest government servants, moneylenders or speculators. . . ."[6]

In 1947, in British India (excluding the Indian states), in fact, 57 percent of the privately owned agricultural land was under the *zamindari* system and highly concentrated in the hands of a few large *zamindars*. In Uttar Pradesh, for example, 1.49 percent of the *zamindars* owned nearly 58 percent of the land. Among them, 804 families or 0.04 percent, held a quarter of the total land in the province. Reliable statistics for Bihar are not available. But the entire state was under permanent settlement, and concentration of land in Bihar was higher than in Uttar Pradesh.

Unlike the English landlords of the eighteenth and nineteenth centuries, moreover, the Indian *zamindars* of British creation were interested primarily in rack renting. They made no effort to improve agriculture, leaving "the land and the tenantry in a plight worse than before." And as a class, they enjoyed "social position, authority, and power out of all proportion to any useful function performed by them in village economy." All of which made them a logical target of nationalist criticism and reform. Declared the Zamindari Abolition Committee for Uttar Pradesh: "There cannot be any permanent and final solution of our food crisis unless landlordism, which must bear the main responsibility for recurrent famines and permanent food scarcity, is done away with . . . . No solution within the existing framework of the land system being possible, the landlord must go . . . the classes and groups that cling to it must disappear."[7]

And so, the *zamindari* system was abolished. But in one of history's most blatant turnabouts, instead of transferring the "land to the tillers"—a key policy slogan at the time—the *zamindars* were elevated to the status of "tillers of the soil." For "personal cultivation" they were given the right to resume virtually as much land as they wanted: "to carve out their own *sir* and *khudkasht* lands, both in respect of location and area. They also got the freedom to resort to large scale evictions of tenants and sharecroppers for this purpose."[8]

By contrast, the oppressed and exploited tenants, provided their holdings were not resumed for "personal cultivation," were required to pay for the right to own the land they had been cultivating.

Ironically, in according the former *zamindar* the right of resumption, the accent was on *"personal* cultivation." Yet to qualify as a "cultivator," he was *not* required to reside in the village, nor even to supervise agricultural operations personally. And if he did absolutely no manual work on the farm, the ruling was that he must still be regarded as a "tiller of the soil." These mythical definitions of "cultivator" and "tiller of the soil" were fabricated because "considerations of social status and caste prejudice prohibit high caste men, Brahmans and Kshattriyas, from engaging in certain kinds of manual work, such as driving the plough which is considered fit only for the lower caste agriculturists or field labourers."[9]

The policy was to ensure that the bigger *zamindars* like Bir Babu in Bihar, 94 percent of whom belonged to the upper three castes of Brahman, Bhumihar, and Rajput, and would therefore not touch a plow, were not hurt by the landmark reform meant to remove their stranglehold on agrarian property and power structure.[10] Thus compounding the original error of the colonial administration in conferring *zamindari* rights on nonagriculturists, hundreds and, in many cases, several thousand acres of land were again handed over gratuitously to the same "feudal" and "parasitic" landlords, with absolute freedom to utilize it as they wished.

In addition, handsome rates of compensation were paid to the *zamindars,* without any discrimination on the basis of accumulated wealth, size of property, or how the title to it had originated. And the land and compensation were given away in this manner because the national government "cannot look with equanimity on the suffering and national waste involved in the forced pauperisation of a section of the people. It is idle talk that the zamindars so released will be absorbed in industrial enterprises, assuming that they are possessed of the aptitude and will to work."[11]

Curiously, their transparent lack of will to work and proven ineptitude in farming—200 years of reckless waste, neglect, and abuse of land—were forgiven and forgotten. Wiped out.[12] On the contrary, the erstwhile nonworking and rack-renting landlords were expected to transform themselves into "owner-cultivators" and substantially step up agricultural production!

Twelve

With Growth and Equity

A galaxy of land reforms followed the abolition of *zamindari* in Bihar and the rest of the country. They did not materially alter the degree of concentration of agricultural land, or the caste and class composition of its owners. Nor ostensibly, the historical differences among landowning communities—in husbandry and the efficiency with which they utilized identical inputs and factors of production.

Output data for crops according to caste, class, income, or farm size groups is not available. But the agro-climatic conditions under which the new high-yielding variety of wheat is grown are fairly uniform in the Indo-Gangetic plain. In fact, better in Bihar, according to the results of experiments conducted by the Indian Council of Agricultural Research. (See table 12.1.)

The structure of tenures also is uniform now. Legally, all landowners are owner-cultivators, though the percentage of land under tenant cultivation in the Punjab is about twice that of Bihar. (See Appendix 4, table 1.) Nevertheless, in the bumper harvest year of 1975–76, the average yield of wheat in Bihar was 1,266 kg per hectare compared to 2,375 kg per hectare in the Punjab. (See Appendix 4, table 2.) The gap in productivity was about the same fifteen years earlier, when farmers had access only to traditional seeds and cultural techniques.

The Green Revolution technology, moreover, was adopted

only, or primarily, by the larger commercial farmers. They own a disproportionately large portion of the cultivated land and other rural assets in the two regions and nationally. (See Appendix 4, tables 3–7.) And the assumption has been that whereas the poor were precluded from improving their output and incomes due to lack of resources, rich landowners like Bir Babu have exhausted the yield and profit potential of the high-yielding varieties. As stated by the National Commission on Agriculture (1976): "On the one side, there will be the *progressive* sector consisting of large farmers who have access to capital and inputs and earn high incomes *through high yields* which make further investment and still higher incomes possible. On the other side, there will remain a large subsistence sector consisting of small farmers, lacking in capital and other resources and having low yields and small incomes."[1] (Italics added.)

Table 12.1   National Demonstrations—Yield of Wheat during 1972*

State	Number of Demonstrations	Yield (q./ha) Mean	Yield (q./ha) Highest	Nutrients applied (kg/ha) N	Nutrients applied (kg/ha) P_2O_5	Nutrients applied (kg/ha) K_2O	Return over operating cost (Rs./ha)
(1)	(2)	(3)	(4)	(5)	(6)	(7)	(8)
Bihar	134	40.56	92.60	116	58	44	3,178
Punjab	163	39.33	59.97	146	66	37	1,507
Uttar Pradesh	433	46.67	72.50	124	55	36	2,983

Source: Indian Council of Agricultural Research.
    *   *Indian Agriculture in Brief*, 14th ed., Directorate of Economics and Statistics (New Delhi, 1975), p. 102.

Yet obviously, "large farmers who have access to capital and inputs" are not necessarily "progressive," earning high incomes through "high yields." The vast differential in crop yields between states and the potential and actual has persisted not because of the impotence of the bottom 46.55 percent of the subsistence cultivators in Bihar who operate less than 0.5 hectare each and a total of 7.53 percent of the cultivated area. It is because a majority of the farmers with medium and large holdings have not utilized their resources to produce more,

more efficiently. It is difficult to understand what prevented them from doing so. Perhaps, they lacked the "inclination" and the "requisite abilities," like the English nobility and owners of large estates of whom Adam Smith wrote: "To improve land with profit, like all other commercial projects, requires an exact attention to small savings and small gains, of which a man born to a great fortune, even though naturally frugal, is very seldom capable. The situation of such a person naturally disposes him to attend rather to ornament, which pleases his fancy, than to profit, for which he has so little occasion."[2]

And so, two hundred years later, in the case of the Bihar gentry also, tractors turned into ornaments, and bullock-drawn plows continued to turn the soil.

Or perhaps, they chose not to strive for larger profits because they, too, did not need to. They have sufficient wealth and income to meet their familial and social obligations, and do not aspire for more. Besides, it is both economic and legitimate for farmers in Bihar and the country to be grossly inefficient—the floor is a bottomless pit—and yet retain possession of the land.

Thus, despite an acute scarcity of arable land and a losing battle between population growth and food production, *anyone* can acquire and own agricultural land, below a not ungenerous ceiling that is seldom enforced. There are no other requirements or conditions.

Consequently, the landowner is free not to cultivate the land personally. Regardless of the climate, quality of the soil, and available technology, he may produce one, two, or more crops in a year. He may also choose not to grow any crop. Let the land lie fallow indefinitely.

Similarly, his yields may be much less than the potential because he may not fertilize the soil adequately. Or not at all—regardless of the price and availability of the nutrients, organic and chemical.[3] Nor need he irrigate the crops, regardless of the differential in yields and access to plentiful supplies of water below the surface, or from a state-owned facility. For the latter, water rates are generally so low that they do not cover even the cost of operating and maintaining the works.

In fact, not only the water for irrigation, but practically

every farm input is subsidized—improved seeds, fertilizers, pesticides, aerial spraying facilities, electricity, credit, and agricultural tools and machinery. The bigger farmers, like Bir Babu and Mohinder Singh, moreover, have little or no difficulty in obtaining the requisite supplies even if there is a shortage.

Aside from the various subsidies, the government guarantees a minimum price now for all the major crops—wheat, rice, millets, sorghum, cotton, jute, sugarcane—accounting for more than 80 percent of the gross crop area. For the wheat harvested in 1978, farmers were assured a year in advance, a support/procurement price of 110 rupees per 100 kilograms. Or approximately, 3.42 U.S. dollars per bushel. Wholesale price index for foodgrains (base 1970/71 = 100) stood at 173.4 in September 1977, and was substantially higher than that of manufactures and other non-farm commodities generally purchased by farm households.

To crown it all, a decade after the introduction of the new seeds, incentive prices and prosperity of the Green Revolution era, the tax on farm incomes was wholly unreal, negligible. Indian agriculture has always been exempt from the central income tax, since it was initiated in 1860. In spite of the considerable wealth of the elite—the top decile of landowners—moreover, for tax purposes, agriculture has been treated as an undifferentiated and disadvantaged sector with a low or no tax-paying ability.

Driven by the need to mobilize more resources for financing development plans, however, some states did impose a provincial tax on agricultural income in addition to the traditional land tax paid by farmers throughout the country. (The incidence of land tax in 1972 was Rs. 4.40 per hectare, or about 50 cents [U.S.].) But the total realized revenue remained insignificant because the tax was very light and the state governments reluctant to displease "the affluent sections of the farm sector, which has benefited the most from the massive investments in agriculture made under the Plans."[4] In 1975, therefore, whereas agriculture accounted for over 45.5 percent of the gross domestic product, the contribution of agricultural revenue—land and income taxes—to the total revenue of the country was a meager 6.1 percent. The ratio of direct taxes to

agricultural incomes, in fact, declined from 1.59 percent in
1960 to 0.7 percent in 1970. (See Appendix 4, table 8.) Five
years later, it was still less than 1 percent. Additional income
accruing to farmers in this period was taxed nominally, or not
at all.

Even in the Punjab, the most prosperous agricultural state
in the country, despite a deficit budget for 1977–78, the
farmers were not required to pay any direct tax on farm income. And the land tax contributed only one percent to the
state's revenue. The cost of collecting it was higher.

In the meantime, the Green Revolution has come and is
practically over.

Although there were considerable variations between
regions, the overall rates of growth for food grains and all crops
were lower during the decade of 1964–65 to 1975–76 than in
the preceding fifteen years—from 1950 to 1965.

Between 1960–61 and 1970–71, the per capita increase in
agricultural production barely kept pace with the growth of
population in the rural areas. In Bihar it declined at a rate of
0.34 percent per year. And even at the end of five years following 1970–71, when the Green Revolution was at the height of
its glory, the agricultural income per head of the rural population as a whole had declined below the 1960–61 level. (See
Appendix 4, tables 9, 10.)

Nevertheless, because of the increase in relative prices in
favor of farm products, rich farmers, like Bir Babu, Mohinder,
and Jaswant, became much richer. But the real income of the
lower strata, of small, subsistence cultivators with little or no
marketable surplus, became still lower.[5] Incidence of rural
poverty increased. (See Appendix 4, table 11.) The landless
agricultural workers, like Shyamlal, generally became poorer;
in larger numbers, in most parts of the country.

Should, then, the development strategy for increasing food
and fiber production continue to be more of the same—yet
more incentives, larger subsidies, even higher prices and
profits, and lower taxes—without taking into account the past
patterns of growth, investment, distribution and usage of land

and other assets among the different sections of farmers in the various parts of the country?

Furthermore, if a decade of high prices, favorable terms of trade, and a profitable and modern technology could not equalize the production conditions for a relatively easy-to-cultivate crop like wheat in even two districts and states, is it likely that any policy based on the incentive theory would materially reduce the wide range of variance that prevails in every other crop and region as well?

It should be clear by now that over 25 years of planned and incremental allocation of development resources for the agricultural cum rural sectors failed to destroy, or even to alter radically, the traditional agrarian structures, institutions, and production arrangements.

It should be equally obvious that a dollar invested in cultivators like Jaswant and Mohinder Singh, belonging to communities with a long and inherited tradition of farming as a profession—every state has them—would yield immeasurably higher returns in terms of produce and productivity than a hundred dollars invested in nonworking landlords of nonagricultural castes, like Bir Babu.

Therein lies the clue, in fact, to why during the past century, the very same prices, techniques, and incentives (or lack of them), that induced a continual expansion of the cultivated area and investment in yield-increasing factors in the Punjab, were never good enough to persuade the farmers in Bihar to invest effort or capital in equal, or even approximate measure, to improve production.

And yet, why should it be so?

If some farm communities are in fact so stubborn and impervious to change, how about the several million men and women in the more recent, so-called modern professions? As for example: officers in the armed forces and enlisted men—the latter mostly peasants. Civil servants, of all ranks. Doctors, lawyers, engineers. Schoolteachers and university professors in the humanities and physical sciences. Manufacturers. And factory workers—a great many of them totally illiterate, straight out of a village. They are drawn from every region, class, creed, caste, culture, and tradition. And although certain groups tend to gravitate toward and excel in particular types of jobs and professions, the great majority appear to have little difficulty in changing their work ethic and habits to conform with a prescribed and, at times, wholly alien mode of conduct. Why is their behavior so strikingly different from that of farmers?

The answer is that unlike the typical peasant, who is generally born into and captive in the calling, the worker entering a nontraditional profession exercises an element of choice, however meager. Even so, and regardless of whether he is rich or poor, educated or not, he is screened for the requisite qualifications, aptitude, and intelligence. If selected, and again, regardless of the rank and status of the job, he (or she) has to undergo a specified type and period of training. Finally, after he qualifies, and for as long as he is permitted or chooses to work in that capacity or career, he is expected to observe a set of institutionalized procedures, rules and regulations, designed to maintain standards of competence and demeanor. To the extent these are not enforced, the operative efficiency of the individual, firm and profession, tends to deteriorate.

And so, if a high caste Hindu decides to enter the modern medical profession, as hundreds of thousands have done since the first medical school was opened in Calcutta in the early nineteenth century, he cannot refuse to perform certain jobs, such as dissecting human flesh, because they are polluting and violate his caste or religious beliefs and customs.

In his personal life, the physician may, and often still does, eat a strict vegetarian diet. He may insist that his college-educated daughter marry within the caste, to a boy of *his* choosing. And if he owns land, he may refuse to cultivate it himself, because caste rules forbid him to touch the plow. But as a practicing surgeon, he cannot hire his traditional counterpart, the barber, or some other menial, to operate on his patients, while he stands by and supervises.

In which case it should not be surprising if the same individual makes an excellent, even brilliant, surgeon; but a miserable farmer.

It is indeed strange that among workers in the organized sectors of the economy, in India and most less developed countries outside the Socialist bloc, *only* the farmer is permitted virtually unrestricted autonomy and freedom of choice from a wide range of production possibilities.

Anyone can own a farm. Even if he is not the son of a farmer. And the only instruction he may ever receive in agronomy, crop or animal husbandry, is occasional ad hoc advice from an extension functionary of doubtful competence and zeal.

Yet not only is the farmer expected to possess or seek out the needed knowledge and information, but over 70 million cultivating households, of whom the majority are illiterate, are assumed to have the motivation and an inborn capacity to make highly complex calculations to allocate, develop, and utilize their resources rationally and efficiently. Evidence to the contrary, of shocking waste and underproduction by even educated farmers, like Bir Babu, is ignored—explained away by mathematical gymnastics, or rejected outright as a reflection on human intelligence and rationality.

Once I ventured to relate the story of Bir Babu, for instance, to an eminent economist at a distinguished American university. His only and spontaneous response was disbelief.

Did I mean to say that the farmer was stupid, irrational?

But then, what are the options?

Is there an alternative strategy that would induce greater efficiency in resource use, an accelerated growth in agricultural production, as well as a greater measure of social and economic equity in the rural sector?

New Directions for a Strategy of Agricultural Development— With Growth and Equity

Only the broad principles of a new strategy can be outlined here. In India, moreover, the choice is limited by two major considerations:

1. The strategy must operate under the democratic federal constitution of the country.

2. Because of the demographic situation, the farm population must be retained in the rural areas. Large-scale migrations to cities must be avoided ahead of alternate employment opportunities.

Commitment to democracy rules out compulsory collectivization of farms on the Chinese or Soviet model. But neither could the free market approach be adopted—the North American model, under which invariably and inexorably, the small, luckless, and the lousy are pushed out and off the land. If India took the latter route, and as a first step, only the small—less than two-hectare farms—were eliminated, some 50 million families would be on the road. Where would they go?

Not only is there practically no scope for reducing the labor force in agriculture.[6] But the rural sector will have to absorb many more workers in the foreseeable future. (See Appendix 4, tables 12, 13.) And no more arable land is available for extension of cultivation.

In which case, the only remaining option is the same as it has been in the past—to persuade a sufficient number of inefficient farmers operating a major portion of the land under each crop to produce more, even if the conditions are not ideal. Change strategies based on education, demonstration, and incentives have not been successful in bringing about the requisite transformation. But it can be done, if farmers also are regarded as normal human beings—neither more nor less stupid, rational or irrational. It means that, as in every other field of economic activity, farmers too must be required to fulfill their obligations to society and maintain certain standards of land use and production. And if they fail to do so, instead of being subsidized, as now, they too must be penalized—for non-use, neglect, or wastage of scarce resources.

Because of the dispersed and atomized structure of agricultural holdings in India, it would be manifestly impossible to enforce specific rules and norms of behavior and performance on individual cultivators, of the kind that the University of Chicago, for instance, imposes on its students and faculty—for admission, promotion, and tenure. Or the United States Steel Corporation—on workers and management. And the market does not perform the normal regulatory function in farming, because cultivators do not compete for the sale of their produce. A particular variety of wheat, rice, and corn fetches exactly the same price, regardless of whether it is grown with or without fertilizers; with or without irrigation; in a soil turned by a hoe, wooden plow, or tractor. Consequently, relative prices can and generally do regulate the allocation of land between different crops and varieties. But not their yields. Nor the intensity of cultivation.

But other, more effective methods could be used to manipulate the production decisions of vast numbers of cultivators of diverse castes, classes, traditions, and history. As for example, the conventional fiscal techniques to render unjustifiably low yields uneconomic and, therefore, infeasible. In essence, by *taxing inefficiency*—as suggested by Jaswant and Mohinder Singh.

Thus the practice of irrigation is probably as old as settled agriculture in the Indian subcontinent. It is vital for saving crops, hence survival, in years of drought. And it is imperative for increasing yields in normal years, even in areas with adequate precipitation. Yet historically, in several parts of the country, there has always been a large lag between availability of water and its usage. Nationally, the lag continues to grow—criminal wastage of a valuable and costly resource.

After a century of experience with the Sone Valley scheme, as well as the more recent projects of Kosi and Gandak in Bihar, however, it should be obvious that extension education alone will not reverse the traditional aversion of most landowners in the region to irrigate winter crops unless the rains fail. Nor is it likely to change materially if the water rates are lowered. They are far too low already.

But the entrenched attitudes and practices will change dramatically, if a heavy fine is imposed on farmers who have access to water but do not irrigate a given variety or crop in the appropriate manner. They should be charged for the quantity of water they do *not* use, at a very much higher rate than what they would pay for using it.

Curiously, Indian planners have never given serious consideration to the possibility of utilizing taxation as a mechanism for accelerating agricultural growth by making it too costly to leave any portion of the cultivable land idle, or to use it below its productive capacity. The general belief is that it would be a disincentive to investment, and that production might, in fact, decline. Even the arguments in favor of taxing the earnings of the well-to-do farmers are usually advanced on grounds of intersectoral or horizontal equity, or the urgent need to raise more resources for development.

And yet, properly structured, tax could be a very efficient instrument or device for inducing radical changes in farm practices and productivity in a short time—far more effective than any strategy tried so far.

The details will have to be worked out by experts. But it would have to be a fixed and steeply progressive tax. Not on incomes. But on the size of holding and potential productive capacity of the soil, valued on the basis of crops, optimum use of land, and the best available technology. The assessment would have to be revised at regular intervals to take into account changes in relative prices and techniques. And it would have to be sufficiently high to insure careful husbandry in every detail—elementary cultural practices, such as seed selection, sowing on time, transplanting on time and in straight rows, composting, weeding—neglect of which is as common today as thatch roofs, flies, and naked children in a typical village.

The country already has a competent, if not incorruptible, revenue administration, and a hoary tradition of land taxes, predating the colonial period. Also the village records and data base. It should not be insuperably difficult, therefore, for the government to administer this new variant of an old levy.

The proposed tax on land will not, however, redistribute rural wealth and incomes. Even if a preemptive estate tax that would compel each generation of the larger farmers to sell some land in order to pay the levy were imposed, structural changes in the distribution of economic assests and power across caste and class lines would still be peripheral. Very gradual—at least in the short run.

If, therefore, as it repeatedly and vehemently professes, the government truly wants an equable distribution of the opportunity and means of agricultural production, there is no other way than to "redistribute." There is no other option.

To do it quickly and simultaneously with rapid growth, moreover, an effective strategy would be to nationalize the land, divide it into a limited range of small size holdings, and then lease the units singly—one to each household prepared to pay the highest rent and work the land with family labor. The leases may be long-term—renewable and inheritable, but with no further subdivision. And they could be terminated, if the farmer wishes to leave, defaults, or violates the terms of the contract. Since the rents would be determined competitively, and competition for land would be keen, the rent would substitute for the proposed land tax and perform the same function—of insuring maximal production.

In one stroke, the reform would resolve some of the most stubborn problems that plague Indian agriculture, for which, again, the land tax cannot be a solution. For example: fragmented holdings would be consolidated, as would be the millions of small plots that can never be viable. The ceiling on landholdings would cease to be a farce. And the nonworking and absentee landlords would be automatically eliminated.

Another very important feature of the scheme would be that the technical and other services, as well as credit, for buildings, equipment, working capital, and so on, would be tied to and determined by the needs of the individual landholding, and not of the cultivator.

Consequently, for the first time in history, the competent and the ambitious among the rural poor would gain equal access to land and the opportunity to cultivate it under the same conditions, incentives, and constraints as the rich—without having to kill them off.

Also for the first time, not only would the traditional caste-based hierarchy of rights and relationships in agricultural production crumble, but a new, dynamic, mobile, and renewable stock of human resources would be created—without prior investments of massive, nonexistent resources in human capital.

Finally, and again for the first time, the reform would establish an egalitarian system of intensive small-scale farming that alone would be appropriate under Indian conditions, resources and factor endowments. Its success in the Far East has been phenomenal.

The Far Eastern model was, in fact, examined by the Agrarian Reforms Committee, appointed by the ruling Indian National Congress party soon after independence. But it was rejected, curiously because it involved hard work. As stated in the committee's report: "The intensive peasant farming of China and Japan with a remarkably high gross yield per acre has not a few advocates in our country. But, it has been universally admitted that peasant farming in China as well as in Japan is characterized by heavy physical labour of small farmers. In China many a farmer does the work even of animals because human labour is cheaper than animal labour."[7]

But then, will the educated and rich landowners, like Bir Babu and Mohinder Singh, agree to pay high taxes or to work small holdings of one to three hectares? Would they not rather quit farming?

To which the answer would be: so much the better, provided they are not permitted to retain ownership of the land. But they would have been offered a fair choice. In any case, *they* will not emigrate to and further crowd the city slums. Or sleep on the pavements of Calcutta. They have enough resources and talent, as well as connections, to invest in other sectors of the economy and flourish. For every hectare thus surrendered, moreover, there will be plenty of other hands willing to till the soil under the new terms and conditions.

Yet, not all the good and successful cultivators will leave. An important reason would be their traditional attachment to the land and village. An even more important reason would be the acute paucity of alternative opportunities. Where would an illiterate farmer like Jaswant go? In which profession, other than farming, could he accomplish as much?[8]

In fact, high taxes and small holdings would be powerful incentives for the good and genuine cultivators to produce as much surplus as possible, even if only to maintain their standard of living. And if they achieve maximum production, and aspire for more, they will pressure for yet better seeds, technology, and services, which would be an impetus for quality and relevant research. Much has been said and written on the subject in recent years. But meaningful research and reforms are generally initiated and implemented in response to the demands of farmers, and not in response to directives from governments and international agencies. Striking variations in the performance of the new land-grant–type agricultural universities in the various states in India reflect this difference in local pressures from their clients on the farms, and not in the organization, or size of investment in plant, staff, and salaries, of the institutions.

In conclusion:

Neither of the proposed policies—of taxation or nationalization of land—would impair the incentives and advantages associated with the family farm.

Nor would they violate human dignity, freedom, and rights of the individual, as commonly understood and accepted in democratic law and ethics.

And they do not denigrate the intelligence or economic rationality of peasants or farmers in India, or the world.

It may be pertinent, perhaps, to recall that modern economic theories and the concept of "rationality" originated in the West. And they were derived, implicitly but essentially, from the Christian belief—that being the children of God, all men have a natural and equal portion of the "light."

Which may be true. But then, it would be equally pertinent to recall that eight out of the ten Commandments to the children of God begin with a categorical: "Thou shalt not. . . ."

And not in Christianity alone. No religion relies solely on the native intelligence and rationality of man to make the obvious choice between a heaven and hell. Yet, judging from the state of human affairs through history, even the collective efforts of the Gods have had only minor success.

Can the high priests of development do better—induce revolutionary changes in the archaic beliefs, attitudes, and farm practices of millions of cultivators, merely by the lure of lush profits or a green paradise on earth?

It is unlikely. Perhaps, impossible. So long at least as farmers like Bir Babu are permitted to own the land without a mandatory obligation to cultivate it efficiently, there cannot be an agricultural revolution—without a revolution.

A Footnote to the History of Wheat in India 1877–1965

I am glad to know that in other directions the agricultural practice of India has improved. The cultivator has always been patient, laborious and skilful, though his methods have been based upon tradition. Latterly the resources of science have been brought to bear upon agriculture and have demonstrated in a very short time the great results that can be secured by its application.
H. M. The King-Emperor, quoted in James Mackenna, *Agriculture in India* (Calcutta: Superintendent Government Printing, 1915).

A favored food, wheat has been cultivated in the northern regions of the Indian subcontinent since prehistoric times. The traditional varieties that were partially replaced by the Mexican dwarfs, however, were not the original native varieties developed through a natural process of selection. They too were developed by scientists and the scientific method.

The Secretary of State for India called for a complete report on Indian wheats as early as 1877. And in 1889, John Augustus Voelcker, Consulting Chemist to the Royal Agricultural Society, was sent to advise on how best to improve the colony's agriculture. Except for chemistry, the agricultural sciences were still in a backward state in England.

An Inspector-General of Agriculture was appointed in 1901. A number of scientists were recruited, and a large government estate was taken over at Pusa in north Bihar to establish a research institute with an experimental farm and agricultural college. In 1906 a detailed plan for systematic work on Indian wheats was drawn up by Albert Howard, research being directed toward genetic manipulation and production of new varieties through a process of cross-breeding and hybridization.

After an exhaustive survey, type specimens of almost every variety were separated, and those with good grain qualities were crossed with English and American varieties to develop new strains with a higher yield potential, better milling quality, rust resistance, and stronger straws. As noted by Howard, aside from want of "strength" and susceptibility to rust, all the indigenous wheats had weak brittle straws, with the result that the crop was often "laid by rain and wind and much damaged."[1] By 1915 the well-known Pusa 12 variety had been fixed as a type, and the first set of Pusa-bred wheats were distributed widely for commercial production.[2]

Internationally, some of the new Pusa varieties were ranked with Manitoba Spring wheats, were in great demand in England, and fetched premium prices. The Indian consumer also accepted them readily. Furthermore, as with the Mexican varieties half a century later, there was little or no problem in persuading wheat farmers to substitute the new seeds for old. Observed the Royal Commission on Agriculture in India: "In no respect has the readiness of the cultivator to accept an improvement the value of which has been demonstrated to him been clearer than in his adoption of improved varieties of crops."[3]

By 1926, the Pusa No. 4 and Pusa No. 12 varieties had spread to every wheat-growing tract in the country, including Bihar. Further work to improve the strains continued. But following the disastrous fall in prices during the depression, it was decided that India should not try to produce more than 9.5 million tons of wheat per year and that there should be no stimulus for extension of acreage.

And so, within half a century, the "traditional" wheats of India were twice transformed. Pusa and the Mexican varieties were developed on separate continents, several decades apart, under very different circumstances and national needs. When the Co-operative Mexican Program was initiated, for example, that country's production was less than 50 percent of its domestic consumption. When the Pusa program was started, although 80 to 90 percent of the produce was consumed locally, India was the third largest exporter of wheat in the world, after Russia and the United States of America. Mexico imported 431,000 tons of wheat in 1944. India exported over 2,000,000 tons in 1904–5.

In the context of the times, and considering the state of

chemical and biological sciences and technology, however, the principles, premises, and assumptions underlying the development of the Pusa and Mexican wheats were strikingly similar. The early British plant breeders also sought maximization of yields and profit. Economic rationality and response of farmers was never questioned, with the logical proviso that "any new variety brought to the notice of the cultivator must yield well under his conditions." That in search of a stronger straw the Pusa scientists overlooked the Norin 10 genes is not surprising. Japan was not a wheat-producing country. And though dwarfs had been developed earlier, Norin 10—the Oriental parent of the Mexican varieties—was registered and released only in 1935. American scientists did not discover it until 1947.

For a similar reason, Pusa wheats could not have been designed for large amounts of chemical fertilizers, in the quantities that the Mexican dwarfs can tolerate. Fertilizers were not available at the time; nor was the manufacturing technology to make their use in grain production profitable. But the importance of nitrogen was clearly understood. And early manurial experiments had demonstrated that, given suitable moisture for germination and growth, nitrogen was the key factor in determining yields.

By 1925, India was manufacturing around 15,000 tons of sulphate of ammonia. But price was still a problem. Under the circumstances, the Pusa wheats were structured for stronger straws, and, unlike the native varieties, they responded to better soil conditions without lodging. As noted by Albert Howard, who with his wife pioneered the wheat-breeding program from 1905–24, "yields of over forty maunds to the acre have already been obtained both on the alluvium in Bihar and also on the black soils of Central India. . . . Some years ago such results would have been considered impossible."[4]

With regard to nitrogen, however, a rough condition of equilibrium had been reached in Indian agriculture. The gains and losses were about equal. To increase crop yields, therefore, the amount of nitrogen added to the soil had to be increased and rendered more effective. After examining various possibilities, Dr. Howard concluded that the only solution lay in more efficient utilization of the manures at the disposal of the cultivator—organic residues of plant and animals. Then, as now, aside from the loss of nitrogen entailed in the burning of cow dung, sufficient use was not being made of the animals' urine, night soil, ashes, crop residues, and so on. And so, he recommended:

> Simple methods, within the means of the cultivator, of composting . . . on the lines adopted so successfully in China and Japan. In these countries intensive agriculture is practiced, and the soil supports a much larger population than India without any importation of artificial manures. The greatest attention is paid in the Far East to the production of organic matter in the right stage of decomposition before it is applied to the fields. It is never used fresh and undecayed, as is often the case in India. Plant residues, in the hands of the peasantry of China, appear to be much more efficacious than they are in India, and it seems well worthwhile exploring the possibility of adapting many of the practices of the Far East to Indian agriculture.[5]

Albert Howard's belief that the Far Eastern practices of conserving and replenishing the soil were relevant and transferable to India persisted. In 1943, *A Note on Technological Possibilities of Agricultural Development,* designed to form the basis of an all-India policy for postwar agriculture, affirmed that the "objection to compost-making, *that it involves labour,* must be got over. If the Chinese cultivator can apply to the land every scrap of available fertilizing material, so can the Indian cultivator."[6] (Italics added.)

But the Indian cultivator never did.

Over the decades, millions of wheat farmers readily exchanged the "old" seeds for "new." But poverty of the soil remained an intractable problem, its enrichment a constant concern. Most of the potential of the improved strains was lost as a consequence, and the country's average yield of wheat (as of most crops) was still one of the lowest in the world in 1960. Later in the decade, when there was a breakthrough in yields, it was not because farmers had adopted the more efficient techniques of soil husbandry of Cathay. It was not necessary. The introduction of the Mexican varieties and advances in the manufacturing process of chemical fertilizers made it economic and profitable for the first time to apply factory-made, ready-to-use nutrients. Compost pits were by-passed by a technology that required more cash but less labor than most Indian farmers were willing to invest in making good farmyard manure. On the outskirts of almost every village and hamlet, therefore, pyramids of cow dung cakes are still stacked for burning and the ground littered with straw, stalks, and rubbish of every description.

Nor did the farmers who wasted organic resources utilize chemical fertilizers with greater efficiency, in the manner and quantity required by the Mexican varieties of wheat. According to the Fifth Five Year Plan, "in the high yielding varieties programme, the application of fertilizer has been around half the recommended dosage in terms of nitrogenous and about 1/3rd in terms of phosphatic and potassic fertilizers."[7] The low level of adoption extended to seed treatment, control of weeds, pests and diseases, and the number of irrigations.

WHAT THEN DID THE GREEN REVOLUTION TRANSFORM?

Conversion Table

Area

1 acre	=	0.40469 hectares
1 hectare	=	2.47109 acres
1 square kilometer	=	0.38610 square miles
1 square mile	=	2.5900 square kilometers

Weight

1 kilogram	=	2.20463 pounds
1 metric ton	=	1,000 kilograms
	=	2,204.63 pounds
	=	26.792 maunds (standard)
1 maund (standard)	=	82.2857 pounds
	=	0.037324 metric tons
1 quintal	=	1.968 hundredweights

Yields

Kilograms per hectare	×	0.892 = Pounds per acre
Quintals per hectare	×	89.218 = Pounds per acre
Hundredweights per acre	×	1.255 = Quintals per hectare
Hundredweights per acre	×	125.54 = Kilograms per hectare

Appendix One

Table 1.1   Bihar and Punjab

Key Indicators	Year	Bihar	Punjab
Total Area (in sq kms)		173,876	50,362
Population (in millions)	1951	38.786	9.134
	1971	56.353	13.551
Density per sq km	1971	324	269
Percentage of rural population to total population	1971	90.00	76.27
Total cropped area (in thousands of hectares)	1971–72	10,683	5,724
Net sown area (in thousands of hectares)	1971–72	8,276	4,076
Area under foodgrains	1972–73	10,126	4,013.3
(in thousands of hectares)	1973–74	9,768.7	4,103.7
Area under cereals	1972–73	8,651.4	3,633
(in thousands of hectares)	1973–74	8,249.6	3,684.8
Total production of cereals	1972–73	8,663.5	7,399.6
(in thousands of metric tons)	1973–74	7,006	7,377.5
Import of cereals	1969–70	824.5	—
(in thousands of metric tons)			
as percentage of production	1969–70	12.80	
Export of cereals	1969–70	—	2,583.9
(in thousands of metric tons)			
as percentage of production	1969–70		39.72

Table 1.1 (continued)	Year	Bihar	Punjab
Import of cereals (in thousands of metric tons)	1970–71	1,048.8	—
as percentage of production	1970–71	14.52	
Export of cereals (in thousands of metric tons)	1970–71	—	2,622.7
as percentage of production	1970–71		39.07

Sources: *Indian Agriculture in Brief*, 14th ed., 1975, pp. 2, 34, 78, 81.
Bihar and Punjab: A Study in Regional Economic Disparity, 1973, pp. 12, 48.

Table 1.2   Land Utilization (in thousands of hectares)

Bihar

	1950–51	1966–67	1968–69	1970–71
Cultivable Area	—	—	11,771	11,797
Total Cropped Area[a]	10,765	9,225	10,898	11,026
Net Sown Area[b]	8,787	7,422	8,325	8,454
Current Fallows[c]	2,199	2,496	1,590	1,573

Punjab

Cultivable Area	—	—	4,276	4,284
Total Cropped Area	4,170	5,171	5,287	5,678
Net Sown Area	3,544	3,870	3,940	4,053
Current Fallows	455	262	208	139

[a]   Total Cropped Area: Includes total cropped area during the year.
If different crops are raised on the same land, it is counted more than once.

[b]   Net Sown Area: Net area under crops; area sown more than once during the year is counted only once.

[c]   Current Fallows: Cultivable land kept uncultivated during the year.

Sources: *Bihar and Punjab: A Study in Regional Economic Disparity*, 1973, p. 22. Government of Punjab, *Statistical Abstract of Punjab, 1974*, pp. 53, 49.

Table 1.3   Index of Productivity in 1970–71
(1955–56 = 100)

	Rice	Wheat
Bihar	125.8	158.6
Punjab	240.3	252.0

Source: *Bihar and Punjab: A Study in Regional Economic Disparity*, 1973, p. 37.

Table 1.4 Farm (Harvest) Price of Wheat in Bihar and Punjab
(Rupees per quintal)

Year	Bihar	Punjab
1960–61	43.99	39.79
1961–62	51.25	41.90
1962–63	42.22	42.76
1963–64	56.45	50.13
1964–65	80.24	56.89
1965–66	90.53	66.63
1966–67	121.13	80.46
1967–68	85.87	78.88
1968–69	87.02	69.27
1969–70	93.25	76.98
1970–71	83.09	76.83
1971–72	81.47	76.16
1972–73	106.72	76.58

Note: Government support and procurement prices would be uniform in the two states. Procurement price for all wheat in 1974–75 and 1975–76 was Rs.105 per quintal as against Rs.71 to Rs.82 for different qualities of the grain in 1973–74. Until 1975–76 no export of wheat, except on government account, was permitted from the producing states. The farmers in Punjab therefore could not benefit from the higher prices in the deficit states.

Sources: *Agricultural Situation in India* (Jan. 1966, Aug. 1967, Aug. 1968, Aug. 1969, Aug. 1970, Aug. 1972, Aug. 1974), pp. 837–38, 592–93, 522, 490, 544, 372, 339. Government of Punjab, *Statistical Abstract of Punjab, 1974,* p. 505. Directorate of Economics and Statistics, *Indian Agriculture in Brief,* 12th ed., 1973, p. 150. Directorate of Economics and Statistics, *Indian Agriculture in Brief,* 14th ed., 1975, pp. 143, 157, 159.

Table 1.5 Fertilizer Consumption, 1974–75
(in thousands of metric tons)

	Nitrogen (N)	Phosphates (P)	Potash (K)	N + P + K
Bihar	79.458	16.279	12.517	108.254
Punjab	228.000	60.000	17.000	305.000

Sources: Directorate of Economics and Statistics, *Indian Agriculture in Brief,* 14th ed., 1975, p. 192.

Table 1.6   Privately Owned Tractors, 1972

	Crawler Tractors		Hand Tractors or
	Up to 75 h.p.	Above 75 h.p.	Power Tillers
Bihar	300	100	400
Punjab	1,200	100	700

	Four-Wheeled Tractors			
	Up to 35 h.p.	36–50 h.p.	Above 50 h.p.	Total
Bihar	3,800	800	400	5,000
Punjab	30,100	8,800	2,300	41,200

Source: Agricultural Implements and Machinery Livestock Census, 1972, pp. 31, 32, 38, 39.

Table 1.7   Tractor-Operated Implements, 1972

	Mouldboard and Disc Plows	Disc Harrows	Cultivators or Tillers	Levelers	Seed cum Fertilizer Drills	Trailers
Bihar	1,400	1,300	4,000	900	200	2,400
Punjab	12,500	15,000	26,700	25,400	9,500	13,900

	Threshers (power-driven)				
	Wheat Threshers	Paddy Threshers	Maize Shellers	Power Chaff Cutters	Other Power-Operated Equipment
Bihar	4,800	2,900	500	2,200	1,000
Punjab	63,500	1,200	8,100	14,400	3,900

Source: Agricultural Implements and Machinery Livestock Census, 1972, pp. 33, 34, 40, 41.

Table 1.8   Plant Protection Equipment, 1972
Sprayers and Dusters

	Hand-Operated	Engine-Operated	Tractor-Operated	Total
Bihar	12,000	800	400	13,200
Punjab	18,300	1,600	700	20,600

Source: Agricultural Implements and Machinery Livestock Census, 1972, pp. 29, 36.

Table 1.9   Bullock and Manually Operated Implements, 1972
(in thousands)

	Plows Wooden	Iron	Blade Harrows	Wet Land Puddler	Earth Leveler or Scrapers	Seed Drills	Maize Shellers	Animal-drawn carts
Bihar	4,055	264	876	260	887	142	5	775
Punjab	654	755	30	35	98	383	15	303

Source: Agricultural Implements and Machinery Livestock Census, 1972,
pp. 28, 35.

Table 1.10   Lift Irrigation Equipment, 1972

	Oil engines with pumpsets used for irrigation			Other agricultural purposes	Total	Electrical pumpsets for irrigation	Persian wheels or Rahats
	up to 5 h.p.	6 to 10 h.p.	above 10 h.p.				
Bihar	38,000	3,000	1,000	7,000	49,000	53,000	53,000
Punjab	151,000	83,000	13,000	3,000	250,000	79,000	51,000

Source: Agricultural Implements and Machinery Livestock Census, 1972,
pp. 30, 37.

Table 1.11   Irrigation Pumpsets/Tube-wells Energized
under Five Year Plans

Number energized ending March...	1951	1956	1961	1966	1969	1974
Bihar	47	697	3,200	10,660	50,005	96,922
Punjab	n.a.	3,095	8,514	25,296	59,112	129,566

Source: Directorate of Economics and Statistics, *Indian Agriculture in Brief*,
14th ed., 1975, pp. 217–18.

Table 1.12   Net Area Irrigated by Tube-wells, Other Wells, Canals,
1971–72 (in thousands of hectares)

		Tube-wells	Other Wells	Canals	Total (from all sources)
	Bihar	394	188	874	2,384
	Punjab	1,186	368	1,369	2,955

Source: Directorate of Economics and Statistics, *Indian Agriculture in Brief*,
14th ed., 1975, pp. 35, 36.

Table 1.13   Irrigation Potential and Utilization from Major and Medium
Irrigation Schemes by March 31, 1972
(in thousands of hectares)

| | Irrigation Potential | | |
	Created	Utilization	Percentage of Utilization to Potential
Bihar*	1,130	689	61
Punjab	778	759	97

*   In terms of the irrigation potential created among the states of India,
    Bihar was second only to Uttar Pradesh. Punjab was seventh.

Source: Planning Commission, Government of India, *Report of Steering Group
          on Fifth Five Year Plan Relating to Agriculture, Irrigation and Allied
          Sectors,* 1973, p. 206.

Table 1.14   Different Types of Motor Vehicles on Road, 1972*

	Motorcars	Jeeps	Motorcycles	Auto-rickshaws
Bihar	19,403	7,715	23,069	164
Punjab	9,050	1,435	16,295	265

*   estimated.

Source: Government of Punjab, *Statistical Abstract of Punjab,* 1974,
          pp. 336, 337.

Table 1.15   Ludhiana/Shahabad

Not all the latest statistics are available yet for the two districts. But the pattern of farmers' investment in Shahabad and Ludhiana is not dissimilar to that in their respective states.

Geographic Area—1972–73
Shahabad—4,408 sq miles
Ludhiana—1,324 sq miles

Net Cropped Area—1972–73
Shahabad—714,971.08 hectares
Ludhiana—323,000 hectares

In 1972–73, Shahabad had 250,000 hectares lying fallow during the *kharif* and 79,000 hectares during *rabi.*
Ludhiana had 1,000 hectares fallow (total) in 1972–73 and *none* at all in 1973–74.

Rainfall
Shahabad—1122.8 mm. (1970–71)*
Ludhiana—570.9 mm. (1967–71)

*   In fifty years, between 1901 and 1950, there were only 6 years when rainfall in Shahabad district was less than 80 per cent of the normal. None of these were consecutive years. In 40 out of the 50 years, the rainfall was between 900 to 1400 mm.

Sources: Directorate of Statistics and Evaluation, Bihar, *Bihar Through Figures, 1971*, p. 12. Government of Punjab, *District Census Handbook—Punjab, No. 11—Ludhiana District,* 1965, p. 2. I.A.D.P. Shahabad, *Agricultural Development in Shahabad,* 1961–72, (Manual), p. 3. Government of Punjab, *Statistical Abstract of Punjab,* 1967, pp. 52, 53. Government of Punjab, *Statistical Abstract of Punjab, 1974*, p. 51. *Punjab Agricultural Handbook, 1974*, p. 7. *District Gazetteer, Shahabad District*, p. 38.

Table 1.16   Area, Production, and Yield of Wheat in Ludhiana District, 1960–73

Year	Area (in thousands of hectares)	Production (in thousands of metric tons)	Yield (in kgs. per hectare)
1960–61	80.5	169.1	1,568.00
1965–66	137.2	338.2	2,230.43
1969–70	226.1	693.3	3,039.22
1970–71	226.4	734.5	3,278.16
1971–72	245.1	815.1	3,310.00
1972–72	253.0	739.5	2,921.25

Source: *Crop Cutting Experiments: Rabi, 1972–73, Intensive Agricultural District Programme Ludhiana* (Punjab: November, 1973), p. 3.

Table 1.17   Net Area Irrigated by Sources, 1969–70
(in hectares)

	Shahabad	Ludhiana
Canals	318,900	30,900
Tanks	36,420	—
Wells (including tube-wells)	78,910	203,800
Other Sources	43,710	—
Total	477,940	234,700

Sources: Directorate of Statistics and Evaluation, Bihar, *Bihar through Figures*, 1971, p. 110. Government of Bihar, *Bihar Statistical Handbook*, 1970, p. 38. Government of Punjab, *Statistical Abstract of Punjab, 1970*, p. 125.

Table 1.18   Fertilizer Distributed
(in metric tons)

	1967–68	1970–71	1973–74
Nitrogenous (in terms of N)			
Shahabad	6,797	16,667	6,107 (up to Jan. 1974)
Ludhiana	11,308	23,067	133,521
Phosphatic (in terms of P_2O_5)			
Shahabad	3,511	6,043	1,456
Ludhiana	4,367	10,339	91,031

Source: Directorate of Economics and Statistics, *Indian Agriculture in Brief*, 14th ed., 1975, pp. 221, 223.

Table 1.19   Implements and Machinery, 1972

	Shahabad	Ludhiana
Tractors	1,235	4,764
Oil engines with pumping sets	1,074	30,696
Electric pumps	6,752	19,902 (for tube-wells only)

Source: I.A.D.P. Shahabad, *Agricultural Development in Shahabad, 1961–72*, (Manual), p. 15. Government of Punjab, *Statistical Abstract of Punjab*, 1974, pp. 129, 130.

Table 1.20   Area, Yield, Production, and Irrigated Area under Wheat
in Shahabad District, 1911–47

	Area (hectares)	Yield (kg./hect.)	Production (metric tons)	Irrigated Area (hectares)
1911–12	85,712	918	78,706	34,531
1912–13	62,443	918	57,338	41,730
1913–14	91,540	1,283	117,477	26,056
1933–34	99,998	830	83,040	28,695
1934–35	100,322	830	83,308	28,821
1935–36	99,715	741	73,904*	33,614
1936–37	98,015	830	81,387	32,305
1937–38	97,853	826	80,804	32,319
1938–39	104,530	786	82,174	32,495
1939–40	103,478	786	81,341	33,782
1940–41	106,675	764	81,492	33,012
1941–42	116,145	742	86,156	33,794
1942–43	116,145	996	115,685	35,863
1943–44	106,756	764	81,526	38,142
1944–45	107,201	786	84,239	38,585
1945–46	106,797	742	79,193	38,588
1946–47	103,761	742	76,942	38,588

*   Crop was damaged due to excessive cold, frost, and cloudy weather.
Yield trends were similar in other wheat-producing districts in
Bihar during this period, though then as now, Shahabad had the
highest acreage under the crop.

Source: *Bulletin on Wheat Statistics in India,* Districtwise, 1972, p. 25.

Table 1.21   Area, Yield, Production, and Irrigated Area under Wheat
in Ludhiana District, 1911–47

	Area (hectares)	Yield (kg./hect.)	Production (in metric tons)	Irrigated Area (hectares)
1911–12	131,074	630	82,577	46,209
1912–13	100,297	923	92,574	38,102
1913–14	103,250	767	79,193	45,361
1933–34	113,723	558	63,457	55,211
1934–35	110,849	1,039	115,172	67,885
1935–36	105,663	1,001	105,769	58,249
1936–37	107,528	1,121	120,539	59,811
1937–38	112,993	1,094	123,614	70,559
1938–39	110,670	993	109,895	73,034
1939–40	98,783	1,071	105,797	71,070
1940–41	108,105	1,054	113,943	69,920
1941–42	112,726	1,073	120,955	75,943
1942–43	117,870	1,194	140,737	73,234
1943–44	113,224	1,075	121,716	80,207
1944–45	114,477	1,059	121,231	76,301
1945–46	110,073	1,000	110,073	69,396
1946–47	115,849	1,023	118,514	76,400

Source: *Bulletin on Wheat Statistics in India,* Districtwise, 1972, p. 62.

Appendix Two

Table 2.1   Procurement Prices of Wheat
(Rupees per maund)

Year	Punjab	Bihar	Uttar Pradesh
1948–49	13.80	—	14.00
1949–50	13.80	14.80	13.80
1950–51	13.00	14.00	14.80–16.00
1951–52	13.00	15.00	14.00–16.00
1952–53	13.00	15.00	14.00–15.00
1953–54	13.00	15.00	Decontrolled

Source: "Food Situation in India, 1939–53," Issued by the Economic and Statistical Adviser, Ministry of Food and Agriculture, Delhi, 1954, pp. xxvi, 96.

Table 2.2   Market Prices of Wheat at Selected Centers
(Rupees per maund)

Year/Month	Moga (Punjab)	Arrah (Bihar)	Chandausi (Uttar Pradesh)
1949			
March	16.80	—	24.00
June	13.96	25.00	19.00
September	13.80	20.00	22.00
1950			
March	13.80	—	16.00
June	13.00	25.00	15.11
September	12.70	26.00	15.10
1951			
March	12.10	26.00	17.80
June	12.80	—	16.30
September	12.80	21.00	17.12
1952			
March	12.12	20.00	16.80
June	13.00	20.00	17.80
September	12.12	23.00	19.80
1953			
March	12.80	18.00	17.80
June	13.80	21.00	16.14
September	13.80	19.80	16.00

Source: "Food Situation in India, 1939–53," pp. 116, 121.

Table 2.3   Average Annual Price of Wheat in Selected States
(Rupees per maund)

State	1952–53	1953–54	1954–55	1955–56	1956–57	1957–58	1958–59	1959–
Bihar	23.21	17.67	14.52	12.29	15.49	16.12	21.94	18.8
Gujerat	21.41	18.44	12.09	14.00	16.50	17.40	19.63	19.6
Punjab	12.91	14.52	13.53	13.01	15.66	14.78	17.05	15.6
Uttar Pradesh	19.29	16.57	12.89	12.10	14.88	15.27	20.48	17.3
Delhi	14.57	15.53	12.47	12.45	15.00	14.92	17.02	15.1
All-India	17.75	16.12	12.78	12.44	15.52	14.99	18.71	16.7

Source: Rath and Patvardhan, *Impact of Assistance Under P.L.480 on Indian Economy,* Gokhale Institute of Politics and Economics (Poona, 1967), p. 148. For prices after 1960, see appendix 1, table 4.

Table 2.4   Net Imports (+) or Exports (−) of Cereals by States, 1947–50
(in thousands of metric tons)

	1947	1948	1949	1950
Bihar	+ 145	+ 104	+ 117	+ 106
Punjab	+ 75	+ 80	+ 64	− 203*
PEPSU	− 29	− 21	− 48	− 109

*   Of the total exports of 203,000 tons, wheat accounted for
         136,000 tons.

Source: "Food Situation in India, 1939–53," pp. 44, 48.

Table 2.5   Production of cereals (in thousands of metric tons)

	Wheat	Total Cereals
1947–48		
All India	5,570	43,741
Bihar	361	3,888
Punjab	820	1,549
PEPSU	218	411
1948–49		
All India	5,650	43,341
Bihar	383	5,139
Punjab	1,002	1,778
PEPSU	262	449
1949–50		
All India	6,290	46,108
Bihar	347	5,013
Punjab	1,196	2,126
PEPSU	320	520
1950–51		
All India	6,360	41,744
Bihar	245	3,461
Punjab	1,062	1,910
PEPSU	264	449
1951–52		
All India	6,085	42,855
Bihar	230	3,808
Punjab	1,242	1,976
PEPSU	409	572

Source: "Food Situation in India, 1939–53," pp. 10–15.

Table 2.6 Linear Rates of Growth in Output, Area, and Productivity
of Wheat in Some of the Districts of Punjab,
1952–53 to 1964–65

District	Output	Wheat Area	Productivity
Ludhiana	8.35	3.70	3.34
Bhatinda	14.19	4.53	6.39
Patiala	13.21	6.39	4.33
Hissar	15.62	12.05	1.44
Mahendragarh	11.91	11.41	0.09
Sangrur	9.55	4.25	3.75
Kangra	6.30	0.69	5.22
Ferozepur	5.28	3.16	1.52
Punjab	6.79	3.92	2.09

Source: "Regional Differences in Crop Output Growth in Punjab,
1952–53—1964–65", Directorate of Economics and Statistics,
(New Delhi, 1967), pp. 12–13.

Table 2.7 Linear Rates of Growth in All-Crop Output in India
and 15 States, 1952–53 to 1964–65

State	Output	Area	Productivity
Punjab*	5.56	2.06	2.86
Gujarat	5.12	0.46	4.52
Tamilnadu	4.91	1.13	3.46
Mysore	4.06	0.83	3.03
Himachal Pradesh	3.93	0.73	3.00
Bihar	3.21	0.71	2.39
Maharashtra	3.19	0.44	2.62
Rajasthan	3.08	3.23	− 0.08
Andhra Pradesh	3.06	0.27	2.72
Madhya Pradesh	2.79	1.35	1.30
Orissa	2.72	0.84	1.78
Kerala	2.52	1.38	1.00
West Bengal	2.07	0.60	1.41
Uttar Pradesh	1.82	0.74	1.01
Assam	1.25	1.32	− 0.07
India	3.42	1.28	1.19

*   Output of rice increased at 12.31%; cotton, 9.35%; sugarcane,
9.28%; potatoes, 19.61%.

Source: "Regional Differences in Crop Output Growth in Punjab,"
pp. 3, 6–7.

Table 2.8   Linear Rates of Growth in All-Crop Output, Area, and
                  Productivity in Seventeen Districts of Punjab,
                  1952–53 to 1964–65

	All Crops		
District	Output	Area	Productivity
Bhatinda	11.32	0.53	10.18
Patiala	10.88	5.83	3.20
Hissar	9.45	3.64	4.27
Karnal	7.25	4.20	2.13
Mahendragarh	6.95	1.30	4.33
Ludhiana	5.95	2.47	2.79
Jullunder	5.41	2.33	2.50
Sangrur	3.99	0.34	3.51
Ferozepur	3.74	0.90	2.52
Hoshiarpur	3.70	1.00	2.48
Rohtak	3.32	0.52	2.58
Ambala	3.10	1.68	1.20
Gurgaon	2.75	1.67	0.92
Amritsar	2.27	1.05	1.17
Kapurthala	1.61	3.52	− 1.28
Kangra	1.35	− 0.51	1.49
Gurdaspur	1.14	0.76	0.42
Punjab	5.56	2.06	2.86

Source: "Regional Differences in Crop Output Growth in Punjab," p. 8.

Table 2.9   Changes in Capital Inputs by Categories and by Source
                  in Punjab

	Percentage Change			
	1950–51	1955–56	1960–61	1964–65
Working Capital	100	114.7	122.5	145.5
Village Source	100	110.9	117.3	118.7
Extra-village source	100	155.2	178.9	441.9
Fixed Capital	100	126.5	141.9	148.8
Village source	100	123.0	134.2	131.5
Extra-village source	100	228.2	371.1	664.4
Total, both sources	100	116.6	125.7	146.6

Source: B. Sen, "Capital Inputs in Punjab Agriculture, 1950–51 to
               1964–65" in *Economic and Political Weekly,* vol. 5, no. 52
               (December 26, 1970), p. A-165.

Table 2.10   Estimate of Working Capital in Punjab Agriculture
(Value in thousand rupees of 1950–51)

Items	1950–51	1955–56	1960–61	1964–65
Seeds	192,529	227,193	232,497	241,790
Feed	423,700	453,720	489,220	486,781
Manures	41,020	48,405	49,535	51,515
Fuel Oil	2,148	6,593	10,636	32,715
Electricity	382	8,049	10,326	32,637
Fertilizer	1,651	11,120	15,282	120,950
Water	52,003	63,300	67,210	77,763
Miscellaneous	4,996	5,896	6,033	6,275
All Items	718,429	824,276	880,739	1,050,426

Source: B. Sen, "Capital Inputs in Punjab Agriculture, 1950–51 to
1964–65," p. A-167.

Table 2.11   Quantity Index of Fixed Capital in Punjab Agriculture
(Base year 1950–51)

Assets	1950–51	1955–56	1960–61	1964–65
Wooden plows	100.0	125.1	117.0	101.2
Iron plows	100.0	171.8	293.1	429.5
Sugarcane crushers:				
power-driven	100.0	114.6	399.1	801.9
bullock-drawn	100.0	117.2	137.4	148.4
Carts	100.0	120.4	138.7	154.9
Wells	100.0	105.5	112.3	117.0
Persian wheels	100.0	105.5	112.3	117.0
Oil engines	100.0	306.9	495.0	1522.6
Electric pumps	100.0	2104.3	2699.7	8532.0
Tractors	100.0	252.7	520.6	924.5
Bullocks	100.0	107.1	115.5	114.9
Index of fixed capital stock	100.0	127.5	142.5	151.0
Depreciated value (Rs million) of capital stock, at constant prices of 1950–51	771.9	983.9	1099.8	1165.8

Source: B. Sen, "Capital Inputs in Punjab Agriculture, 1950–51 to
1964–65," p. A-168.

Table 2.12   Distribution of Net Investment per Farm under Various Heads in Different Regions of Bihar (in Rupees)

	North Bihar		South Bihar	
	Amount	Percent of total	Amount	Percent of total
Purchase of land	86	35.5	81	42.6
Purchase of livestock	57	23.4	58	30.5
Purchase of implements, machinery and equipment, etc.	11	4.5	7	3.7
Construction and repair of farmhouse	89	36.6	34	18.0
Bunding and other land improvements, including land reclamation	—	—	7	3.7
Development of irrigation resources	—	—	—	—
Laying of orchards and plantation	*	—	3	1.5
Total	243	100.0	190	100.0

* Less than one.

Source: C. P. Shastri, "Investment of Farm and Capital Formation in Agriculture with Particular Reference to Bihar," in *Indian Journal of Agricultural Economics,* vol. 20, no. 1 (January–March, 1965), p. 180.

Appendix Three

Table 3.1a   Number of Wells in Use in the Punjab (1889–1900)

Year	Number of Wells			Area of Crops Matured by Well-Irrigation (acres)
	Masonry	Temporary	Total	
1889–90	219,940	42,660	262,600	3,959,427
1899–1900	274,851	73,859	348,710	4,154,598

Source: *Report of the Indian Irrigation Commission, 1901–3, part 2, The Punjab* (Calcutta, 1903), p. 30.

Table 3.1b   Gross Area Irrigated from Different Sources in Ludhiana

Ludhiana	1898–99 (in acres)	1899–1900 (in acres)	1900–1901 (in acres)	Number of wells in use in 1899–1900	
Canals (govt.)	71,601	95,855	66,257	Masonry	9,924
Canals (private)	—	—	—	Temporary	1,536
Tanks	548	647	176	Total	11,460
Wells	180,190	200,273	127,465		
Total	252,339	296,775	193,898		
Other sources	—	—	—		

Source: *Report of the Indian Irrigation Commission, 1901–3*, p. 371.

Table 3.2 Costs and Returns of Major Irrigation Works in the Punjab and Bihar, (1900–1902)

Name of Works	Area irrigated annually (in thousands of acres)	Capital cost (in lakhs of rupees)	Gross Revenue (in lakhs of rupees)	Net Revenue (in lakhs of rupees)	Returns on Capital		
					Direct	Indirect	Total
Punjab major works (1900–1901)	4,357*	920.76	146.16	103.14	11.2	4.0	15.2
Sone Canals in Bihar—average for 3 years ending 1901–1902	481	267.52	11.12	5.07	1.9	1.0	2.9

*   Exclusive of 286,000 acres irrigated on Native States branches of Sirhind Canal and Patiala section of Sirsa Branch, Western Jumna Canal.

Source: *Report of the Indian Irrigation Commission*, 1901–03, part 1, p. 28.

Table 3.3   Agricultural Production in the Punjab, (1898–1914)

	1898–99	1903–4	1908–9	1913–14
Wheat (tons in lakhs)	19.78	30.75	30.62	31.89
Rape and mustard (in thousands of tons)	56.0	159.2	183.9	165.0
Cotton (bales of 400 lbs.)	138,926	261,241	324,000	612,000

Source: *Area and Yield of Crops in India.*

Appendix Four

Table 4.1   Variations in Extent of Tenancy
(in thousands of hectares)

States	Total cultivated area	Total leased-in area	Percent of leased-in area to cultivated area
Bihar	8,237	1,194	14.5
Punjab	2,806	788	28.1
Total	130,095	13,819	10.6

Source: NSS census of landholdings, 1971–72.

Table 4.2   Wheat and Rice Yields in Bihar and Punjab (kg./hectare)

	1950–51	1960–61	1968–69	1970–71	1972–73	1973–74	1975–76*
Wheat							
Bihar	437	747	1,150	957	1,250	1,236	1,266
Punjab	1,042	1,237	2,177	2,238	2,233	2,216	2,375
Rice							
Bihar	455	865	957	788	947	802	922
Punjab	956	1,035	1,364	1,765	2,008	2,287	2,553

*   1975–76 was a year of record output of foodgrains totaling 120.83 million metric tons nationally.

Source: Directorate of Economics and Statistics, Ministry of Agriculture and Irrigation.

Table 4. 3   Operational Landholdings in Bihar
              (4 hectares and above)

Size	Holdings (percent)	Holdings (in thousands)	Area (percent)	Area (in thousands of hectares)
4 hectares and above	8.94	678.7	48.18	5,535.5
5 hectares and above	5.99	455.3	39.56	4,546.7
10 hectares and above	1.77	135.1	20.54	2,360.1
10 to 20 hectares	1.38	105.4	12.12	1,392.1
Above 20 hectares	0.39	29.7	8.42	968.0

Source: Agricultural Census of Bihar, 1970–71.

Table 4. 4   Operational Landholdings in Bihar
              (2 hectares and less)

Size	Holdings (percent)	Holdings (in thousands)	Area (percent)	Area (in thousands of hectares)
2 hectares and less	78.98	5,982.5	29.71	3,407.8
0.5 to 0.99 hectares	17.79	1,347.5	8.56	979.7
1.0 to 2.0 hectares	14.64	1,109.1	13.62	1,562.9
Less than 0.5 hectares	46.55	3,525.9	7.53	865.2

Total number of holdings: 7,577,200
Total area: 11,480,000 hectares
Average area per holding: 1.52 hectares

Source: Agricultural Census of Bihar, 1970–71.

Table 4. 5   Number of Operational Holdings and Area Operated
in the Punjab, 1971

Size (in hectares)	Number of Holdings	Area Operated (in hectares)
Below		
0.5	310,049	77,100.28
0.5–0.99	207,519	148,155.38
1.00–1.99	260,083	372,130.78
2.00–2.99	169,826	412,227.76
5.00–9.99	168,734	1,163,513.46
10.00–19.99	58,498	770,506.79
20.00–29.99	7,631	180,768.18
30.00–39.99	1,801	61,089.31
40.00–49.99	652	28,893.89
50.00 and above	301	26,114.89
Total	1,375,392	3,974,090.76

Source: The Third Decennial World Agricultural Census 1970–71, Report
for Punjab State, parts 1 and 2 (Government of Punjab,
Chandigarh, 1974), table 1.

Table 4. 6   National Agricultural Census Estimate of Operational
Landholdings, 1970–71

Size (in hectares)	Number of holdings (in thousands)	Operated Area (in thousands of hectares)	Average size (in hectares)
0.002–1.00	35,682 (50.62)	14,545 (8.97)	0.41
1.01–2.02	13,432 (19.05)	19,282 (11.89)	1.43
2.03–4.04	10,681 (15.15)	29,999 (18.50)	2.81
4.05–10.12	7,932 (11.25)	48,234 (29.75)	6.08
10.13 and above	2,766 (3.92)	50,064 (30.88)	34.40
Total	70,493 (100.00)	162,124 (100.00)	2.30

Figures in parentheses indicate percentage distribution.

Table 4. 7   Pattern of Asset-Holdings of Rural Households, 1971–72

Decile Group	Percentage Share in the Aggregate Amount		
	Bihar	Punjab	
0–10	0.19	0.05	
20–30	0.94	0.35	
40–50	2.23	1.03	
70–80	8.28	5.16	
80–90	15.00	11.17	
90–100	62.93	76.73	All India
97.5–100	36.33	51.99	35.20
99–100	23.88	37.45	22.96

Source: All India Debt and Investment Survey, 1971–72.

Table 4. 8   Net Domestic Product Originating in Agriculture and Direct Tax Burden on Indian Agriculture, 1960–61 through 1969–70

Year	NDP originating in agricultural sector (Rs. crores)*	Direct taxes on agriculture (land revenue and income tax) (Rs. crores)	Ratio of taxes to incomes	Ratio of change in taxes to change in income
1960–61	67,070	1,067	1.59	
1961–62	70,100	1,046	1.49	− .007
1962–63	71,960	1,296	1.80	.134
1963–64	84,730	1,327	1.56	.003
1964–65	101,550	1,305	1.28	− .001
1965–66	98,010	1,218	1.24	.025†
1966–67	115,950	1,001	0.86	− .012
1967–68	130,000	1,080	0.83	.005
1968–69	150,000	1,140	0.75	.003
1969–70	158,000	1,160	0.70	.002

*   one crore = 10 million
†   Ratio of decreased taxes on decreased income.

Source: Barla, C. S.: *Agricultural Taxation and Economic Development*, (mimeographed), Department of Agricultural Economics, Michigan State University, East Lansing, 1970.

Table 4.9   Regional Distribution of Agricultural Growth

Region	Rural population, 1960–61 (in millions)	Agricultural income per rural person, 1960–61 (Rs million)	Annual rate of growth of agricultural income per person, 1960–61 to 1970–71
Punjab, Haryana, Gujerat, Karnataka, Rajasthan*	65.4	216	2.10%
Rest of the country	294.9	175	− 0.35%
All India	360.3	183	0.22%

*   These states covered only 18 percent of the rural population.

Table 4. 10   Agricultural Growth in Selected States

States	1960–61 Rural population* (in thousands)	Per capita NDP (Rs.)	1970–71 Rural population* (in thousands)	Per capita NDP Agr.†	Annual per capita growth 1960–61 to 1970–71 (percent)
Rajasthan	16,874	187	21,222	247	2.82
Punjab	8,568	290	10,335	377	2.66
Haryana	6,283	265	8,264	331	2.25
Gujerat	15,317	208	19,201	246	1.69
Karnataka	18,320	197	22,177	228	1.47
Uttar Pradesh	64,275	164	75,953	180	0.94
Andhra Pradesh	29,709	189	35,100	202	0.67
Tamil Nadu	24,696	211	28,734	209	− 0.10
Bihar	42,534	118	50,719	114	− 0.34
West Bengal	26,385	199	33,345	186	− 0.67
Maharashtra	28,391	224	34,701	149	− 4.00
All India	360,298	183	439,046	187	

    *   1961 and 1971.
    †   In 1960–61 prices.
Sources: Census of India, 1971, part 2A (i)—general population tables.
                R. P. Katyal and V. K. Sood, "Real Growth in Agriculture
                at State Level," Indian Association for Research in National Income
                and Wealth, Tenth General Conference, January 1976.

Table 4.11   NSS Estimates of Incidence of Poverty in Rural India

Year	Price Index for Poor*	Poverty Line (Rs. per capita for 30 days)	Incidence of Poverty (percentage poor)	Rural per capita Consumption (in 1960–61 prices)†
1960–61	100	15.0	38.9	21.47
1963–64	118	17.7	44.5	21.51
1964–65	142	19.8	46.8	18.62
1967–68	206	30.9	56.5	16.21
1970–71	192	28.8	47.5	18.39

* The price index is based on the Consumer Price Index for Agricultural Laborers.

† Obtained by using the Price Index of the Poor as the deflator to be applied to consumption per capita in rural areas as reported in the National Sample Survey.

Table 4.12   Population Growth

Year	Total Population (millions)	Decade Increase (percent)	Average Annual Increase (percent)	Urban (percentage)
1901	238.3			10.83
1911	252.0	5.73	0.56	10.29
1921	251.1	(− 0.30)	—	11.18
1931	278.9	11.00	1.05	12.00
1941	318.5	14.23	1.34	13.86
1951	361.0	13.31	1.26	17.30
1961	439.1	21.64	1.98	17.98
1971	547.9	24.80	2.24	19.91

Source: Government of India, Office of the Registrar General, *Pocketbook of Population Statistics* (New Delhi, 1972).

Table 4.13   An Illustrative Projection of the Labor Force*

	Labor Force		Quinquennial Increments			
Year	Millions	As Percent of Population	Period	Million	Percent	Average Annual Growth
1971	219.3	39.4	1971–76	29.0	13.2	2.48
1976	248.3	40.2	1976–81	33.8	13.6	2.55
1981	281.2	41.6	1981–86	37.0	13.1	2.46
1986	319.1	43.4	1986–91	37.6	11.8	2.23
1991	356.7	45.0	1991–96	38.6	10.8	2.05
1996	395.3	46.9	1996–2001	36.8	9.3	1.78
2001	432.1	48.9				

*   On the assumption that labor participation rates will remain
constant at 1972–73 level.

Source: The projections were prepared by the South Asia region division
of the World Bank in 1977.

Notes

Intro-
duction

1 W. David Hopper, "The Promise of Abundance," in *Regional Semi-nar on Agriculture: Papers and Proceedings* (Manila: Asian Development Bank, 1969), pp. 30, 31.

2 *Report of the National Commission on Agriculture, 1976,* part 1, "Review and Progress," (New Delhi: Ministry of Agriculture and Irrigation), chap. 1, appendix 3.15.

3 Ibid., p. 542.

4 Biplab Dasgupta, "India's Green Revolution," in *Economic and Political Weekly,* Annual Number, (Bombay, February 1977), p. 242.

5 *Government of India Economic Survey 1975–76* (New Delhi: 1976), pp. 6,7.

6 The exact number of paddy cultivators is not known. But rice is the most extensive single crop in India, cultivated on close to 40 million hectares.

7 Sitaram Yechuri, "Inter-State Variations in Agricultural Growth Rate, 1962 to 1974," in *Economic and Political Weekly, Review of Agriculture,* (Bombay, December 1976), p. A-153.

8 Crop cutting experiments in 1970–71 and 1971–72 showed that compared to unirrigated crops, yields of irrigated paddy were higher by about 80 to 95 percent; and of wheat by 105 to 115 percent. Irrigated cotton produced about three times as much as unirrigated cotton. See *Report of the National Commission on Agriculture, 1976,* part 1, "Review and Progress," p. 603.

9 See R. P. Pathak, K. R. Ganapathy, Y. U. K. Sarma, "Shifts in Pattern of Asset-Holdings of Rural Households, 1961–62 to 1971–72," in *Economic and Political Weekly,* vol. 12 (Bombay, March 19, 1977), pp. 507–17.

10 Gary S. Becker, *The Economic Approach to Human Behavior* (Chicago: The University of Chicago Press, 1976), p. 7.

11   Ibid., p. 7.
12   *Asian Agricultural Survey 1976, Rural Asia: Challenge and Opportunity* (Provisional Printing, Asian Development Bank, 1977), p. 82.
13   For a fuller discussion, see chap. 12, p. 88 ff. Also see, Nair, *The Lonely Furrow: Farming in the United States, Japan, and India* (Ann Arbor: The University of Michigan Press, 1969), pp. 231–34.

Chapter   1   P. C. Roy Chaudhury, *Bihar District Gazetteers: Purnea* (Patna, India:
One   The Superintendent Secretariat Press, 1963), p. 172. Also see pp. 1, 2, 114, 417, 270.
           2   Ibid., p. 286. Also see pp. 82–83, 86, 89.
           3   Ibid., p. 286.
           4   Ibid., p. 286. Also see pp. 3, 287, 493, 502. And see Tomasson Jannuzi, *Agrarian Crisis in India: The Case of Bihar* (Austin, Texas: University of Texas Press, 1974), pp. 10, 11.
           5   Ibid., p. 419. Also see p. 286.
           6   Ibid., p. 410.
           7   Ibid., pp. 418, 419.
           8   Ibid., p. 421. Also see pp. 287, 502, 493.
           9   Ibid., p. 425.
          10   Ibid., p. 530.
          11   Ibid., p. 630. The couplet says: "if you want to die, do not take poison. Go to Purnea."

Chapter   1   Roy Chaudhury, *Bihar District Gazetteers: Purnea,* pp. 112–13, 168.
Two   2   Ibid., p. 132.
               Census Report, Bihar and Orissa, 1921; Quoted in Birendranath Ganguli, *Trends of Agriculture and Population in the Ganges Valley* (London: Methuen, 1938), p. 136.
           4   Roy Chaudhury, *Bihar District Gazetteers: Purnea,* p. 173.
           5   Ibid., p. 204.

Chapter   1   Only 1.03 percent of the operational holdings were of 50 acres and
Three   more according to the Government of India—National Sample Survey, Seventeenth Round, September 1961–July 1962.
           2   Sudhir Sen, *A Richer Harvest* (New Delhi, India: Tata McGraw-Hill, 1974), p. 206.
           3   Kusum Nair, *Blossoms in the Dust* (London: Gerald Duckworth, 1961; New York: Praeger, 1961), pp. 100–101.

Chapter   1   Edward S. Mason, *Economic Development in India and Pakistan;* Occa-
Five   sional Papers in International Affairs, number 13 (Cambridge, Mass.: Harvard University, 1966), p. 8. Also see page 7.
           2   K. N. Raj, *Indian Economic Growth: Performance and Prospects* (New Delhi: Allied Publishers, 1965), pp. 4, 11.

3   C. Subramaniam, *India of my Dreams* (Bombay: Orient Longman, 1972), pp. 16, 113.
4   Ibid., pp. 117, 119.
5   Theodore W. Schultz, "Food for the World: Economic Implications and Opportunities." Paper presented at the Ninth Agricultural Industries Forum, University of Illinois, February, 1967 (mimeographed), p. 2
6   Theodore W. Schultz, *Transforming Traditional Agriculture* (New Haven, Conn.: Yale University Press, 1969). See pp. 5, 33, 105, 115, 168.

Chapter Six

1   See *Report on the Analysis of Crop Cutting Experiments, Rabi, 1972–73,* Information Unit, Intensive Agricultural District Programme (Ludhiana, November 1973), pp. 6, 9, 10.

Chapter Eight

1   *Fifth Five Year Plan, 1974–79 (Agriculture),* Directorate of Agriculture, Bihar (mimeographed), pp. 13, 69.
2   In 1968–69, Punjab produced 4,491,000 metric tons of wheat on 2,063,000 hectares, of which 57.20% was under the high yielding varieties.
3   *Report of the Indian Irrigation Commission, 1901–03,* part 2 (India: Superintendent Government Printing, 1903), p. 156.
4   *Agricultural Development in Shahabad, 1961–1972,* Intensive Agriculture District Programme (mimeographed), p. 1.
5   Finucane, *Report on the Cultivation and Trade of Wheat in India,* Calcutta, 1886, cited in Albert and Gabrielle L. C. Howard, *Wheat in India,* published by the Imperial Department of Agriculture in India (Thacker, Spink and Co., 1909), p. 17.
6   Dorris D. Brown, *Agricultural Development in India's Districts* (Cambridge, Mass.: Harvard University Press, 1971), p. 90.
7   *Agricultural Development in Shahabad, 1961–1972,* p. 21.
8   The yield of wheat in Ludhiana in 1913–14 was a paltry 767kg, and 3,310 kg per hectare in 1971–72. Due to a change in the method of computing yields from "eye-estimation" to random crop-cutting surveys with effect from 1948–49, however, the statistics for both Shahabad and Ludhiana after 1948 are not strictly comparable with those of earlier years. But even prior to the change, for a decade and a half, between 1933–48, wheat yields in Shahabad were consistently lower than in 1911–14. By 1946–47, the acreage under wheat had increased, but production had declined. (See appendix 1; tables 20, 21).
9   M. L. Dantwalla, Preface to *Comparative Experience of Agricultural Development in Developing Countries of Asia and the South-East since World War II,* Papers and Proceedings of International Seminar held at New Delhi, October 1971, The Indian Society of Agricultural Economics (Bombay: Thacker and Co., 1972), p. 40, 41.

Chapter 1 Tarlok Singh, *Towards an Integrated Society* (Westport, Conn.:
Nine   Greenwood Pub. Co. 1969), p. 234.
        2 *Report of the Indian Irrigation Commission, 1901–1903*, part 2 (India:
            Superintendent Government Printing, 1903), pp. 157, 161–62.
        3 Supplies of groundwater are much poorer in the Punjab than in
            Bihar. In 1955–59, of the 18,000 sq km explored in each state for
            development of groundwater by heavy-duty tube-wells, 2,600 sq km
            had "highly productive" aquifers in the alluvial plains of Bihar,
            compared to only 1,000 sq km with "productive" aquifers in the
            composite state of Punjab. See *Indian Farming*, January 1973, vol.
            22, no. 10 (Delhi: R. B. Jain), p. 6, table 1.
        4 *Report of the Irrigation Commission, 1972*, vol. 2, Ministry of Irrigation
            and Power, New Delhi, p. 73.
        5 Ibid., pp. 72–73.
        6 Ibid., p. 65.

Chapter 1 *Report of the Irrigation Commission, 1972*, vol. 2, Ministry of Irrigation
Ten   and Power, New Delhi, pp. 75, 76; vol. 3, p. 116, table 6.3.
        2 *Report of the Indian Irrigation Commission, 1901–3*, part 2 (India:
            Superintendent Government Printing, 1903), p. 156.
        3 Ibid., p. 157.
        4 Ibid., p. 157.
        5 Ibid., p. 177.
        6 Ibid., p. 177.
        7 Ibid., p. 178.
        8 Ibid., p. 3.
        9 Ibid., part 1, p. 40.
       10 Ibid., part 2, p. 33.

Chapter 1 Industry and Trade, p. 40–41, cited in H. Calvert, *The Wealth and
Eleven   Welfare of the Punjab* (Lahore, 1922), p. 70.
        2 S. S. Thorburn, *Mussalmans and Money-lenders in the Punjab* (London:
            William Blackwood and Sons, 1886), p. 37.
        3 H. Calvert, *Wealth and Welfare of the Punjab*, p. 140.
        4 Ibid., p. 140.
        5 A sample survey in the Punjab of "large farms"—of more than eight
            hectares each—in 1967–68, showed that 84.06 percent of the farm-
            ers were Jat Sikh. See Ashok Rudra, "Big Farmers of Punjab," in
            Economic and Political Weekly, Review of Agriculture. vol. 4, (Bombay,
            December 1969), p. A-213, table 2.
        6 *Report of the United Provinces Zamindari Abolition Committee*, vol. 1
            (Allahabad, 1948), p. 340.
        7 Ibid., p. 357.
        8 *Report of the National Commission on Agriculture*, part 15 (Agrarian

Reforms), Ministry of Agriculture and Irrigation, (New Delhi, 1976), p. 73.

9   *Zamindari Abolition Report,* p. 365.

10 Ninety-two percent of the agricultural laborers belonged to the scheduled castes, scheduled tribes, and the middle and low castes. *Rural Manpower and Occupational Structure,* Agricultural Labour Enquiry, Ministry of Labour, Government of India (New Delhi, 1954).

11 *Zamindari Abolition Report,* p. 399.

12 By 1973 not a single acre in Bihar had been distributed or even declared surplus as a result of the Ceiling Area and Acquisition of Surplus Land Act of 1961 as amended in 1971 fixing a limit of ten to thirty acres (depending on quality) per member of the family.

Chapter Twelve

1   *Report of the National Commission on Agriculture,* part 2 (Policy and Strategy), Ministry of Agriculture and Irrigation, (New Delhi, 1976), p. 82.

2   Adam Smith, *The Wealth of Nations,* ed. Edwin Cannan, (Chicago: The University of Chicago Press, 1976), book 3, p. 410.

3   In Bihar, although the acreage sown to the high-yielding varieties— wheat, rice, maize—increased from 99,500 hectares in 1966–67 to an impressive 2,550,000 hectares in 1973–74, the consumption of chemical fertilizers increased by only 0.1 kg per cropped hectare— from 9.0 kg in 1966 to 9.1 kg in 1974.

4   *Government of India Economic Survey 1975–76* (New Delhi, 1976) p. 27.

5   On the average the small farms, of 2.5 acres or less, sell 24.5 percent of their output and produce 9.5 percent of the total production.

6   According to the 1971 census the total labor force numbered 180.3 million. Agriculture claimed 72.0 percent of the total or 129.9 million workers. Of these 26.3 percent or 47.49 million were classified as agricultural labor.

7   *Report of the Congress Agrarian Reform Committee,* published by the All-India Congress Committee (New Delhi, 1949), p. 20.

8   For more than two generations now farmers in Japan have all been to school. Both prior to the postwar land reform and since, the overwhelming majority of the cultivators were operating less than 1.5 hectare per household. Even in the mid-sixties moreover, the average Japanese cultivator put in 50 times the number of hours as an American farmer in California to produce the same quantity of rice, and about four times more labor per hectare than the paddy cultivator in India. See Kusum Nair, *The Lonely Furrow,* pp. 195, 227, 294 note 15.

History of Wheat in India

1   For a general description see James Mackenna, *Agriculture in India* (Calcutta: Superintendent Government Printing, 1915), pp. 40, 41.

2   The improved varieties are designated by numbers. When the Insti-

tute was located at Pusa, the word "Pusa" was prefixed to the numbers. After the Institute moved to New Delhi in 1936, the prefix was changed to Imperial Pusa and the varieties designated as "I.P.4," etc. Since 1947, the words "New Pusa" or "N.P." are being prefixed to the same numbers. Thus, "Pusa 4," which later became "I.P.4," is now designated as "N.P.4."

3   *The Royal Commission on Agriculture in India* (Bombay: The Government Central Press, 1928), pp. 94, 95.

4   Albert Howard, *Crop Production in India: A Critical Survey of its Problems* (Humphrey Milford, Great Britain: The Oxford University Press, 1924), pp. 68, 107, 108.

5   Ibid., p. 39.

6   W. Burns, *Technological Possibilities of Agricultural Development in India* (Lahore: Government Printing Press, 1944), p. 121.

7   *Draft Fifth Five Year Plan,* 1974–79, vol. 2 (Government of India, Planning Commission), p. 4.

Glossary

Ahar	a natural pond used for irrigation.
Babujee	a term often used for father. Can also refer to a superior or clerk.
Begar	compulsory free labor which peasants were obliged to provide to the landlord or the state.
Benami	clandestine transfer of property to relatives and others through fictitious or collusive transaction.
Bania	of Vaisya caste; generally the village shopkeeper and moneylender.
Batai	sharing of grain produce in lieu of rent or revenue.
Bataidar	sharecropper.
Bet	low-lying riverain land.
Chakki	hand-worked millstone for grinding corn and other grains.
Chana	gram; chick-pea or pulse.
Charpoy	a string bed with wooden frame.
Deorhi	dwelling or house.
Desi	native or indigenous.
Dhoti	common male garment in India.
Garibi hatao	*garibi* means poverty and *hatao* means remove.
Ghee	clarified butter.
Gud	brown, unrefined sugar made from sugarcane juice.
Harijan	untouchable or one of the scheduled castes as classified in the Indian Constitution.
Khaddar	handspun and handwoven cloth.
Kharif	monsoon or autum crop.
Khatians	legal ownership papers.

Khudkasht	hereditary land allegedly cultivated by a resident owner. In Bihar, except for a small area around the dwelling, the landlords used to almost invariably sublet the land to tenants.
Lale	shopkeepers or traders; used here to mean nonagriculturists.
Langoti	loincloth.
Lassi	buttermilk.
Mukhia	chief; also a title for the president of the village council.
Pains	irrigation ditches.
Panchayat	elected village council.
Pan-chayati raj	system of local self-goverment.
Patloon wallah	a person wearing pants, Western style.
Patwari	village accountant for maintaining village records of rights in land and of land revenue.
Pucca	solid; also a structure of brick or concrete.
Rabi	winter or spring crop.
Rayat	*ryot,* or *raiyat.* Farmer or peasant; generally used to indicate ownership of an interest in land held directly from the state.
Roti	Indian-style unleavened bread.
Sahukar	professional moneylender.
Sir	the term is applied to land cultivated by the hereditary proprietor or *zamindar* as his own special land, either by hired labor or tenants at will.
Swaraj	independence from British rule.
Tarkari	cooked vegetable.
Tehmat	the traditional sarong-style male dress in the Punjab.
Thana	subdivision of a district for administrative and land revenue purposes.
Zamindar/ Zamin-dari	A superior form of land interest created in several parts of India under the Permanent Settlement of 1793, under which the holder of the interest or *zamindar* acted as an intermediary of the state in the collection of rents and paid a fixed sum of land revenue to the government. In the Punjab, the term denotes simply a landowner, however small.

Bibliography

Arrow, Kenneth J. *Economic Development: The Present State of the Art*. East-West Communications Institute. Paper no. 14. Honolulu: East-West Center, October, 1975.

Arrow, Kenneth J. *Social Choice and Individual Values*. Cowles Foundation Monograph 12. New Haven and London: Yale University Press, 1975.

Asian Agricultural Survey. Published for the Asian Development Bank by University of Washington Press, 1969.

Asian Agricultural Survey 1976. Rural Asia: Challenge and Opportunity (Provisional Printing). Asian Development Bank, 1977.

Baden-Powell, B. H. *Land Revenue and Tenure in British India*. London: Clarendon Press, 1913.

Barla, C. S. *Agricultural Taxation and Economic Development*. Mimeographed. East Lansing, Mich.: Department of Agricultural Economics, Michigan State University, 1969.

Barrier, Norman G. *The Punjab Alienation of Land Bill of 1900*. Program in Comparative Studies on Southern Asia. Monograph no. 2. Duke University Commonwealth-Studies Center. Duke University, 1966.

Becker, Gary S. *The Economic Approach to Human Behavior*. Chicago: University of Chicago Press, 1976.

Bhatia, Jatinder. "Agricultural Land Taxation in Punjab." *Economic and Political Weekly*, vol. 4, no. 3. January 18, 1978.

Bhatt, Mahesh. "How Good a Tax is Agricultural Income

Tax?" *Economic and Political Weekly,* vol. 4, no. 22, May 31, 1969.

Bhutani, V. C. *The Apotheosis of Imperialism, Indian Land Economy Under Curzon.* New Delhi: Sterling Publishers, 1976.

Blyn, George. *Agricultural Trends in India, 1891–1947: Output, Availability, and Productivity.* Philadelphia: University of Pennsylvania Press, 1966.

Brown, Dorris D. *Agricultural Development in India's Districts.* Cambridge: Harvard University Press, 1971.

Burns, W. *Technological Possibilities of Agricultural Development in India.* Lahore: Government Printing Press, 1944.

Calvert, H. *The Wealth and Welfare of the Punjab.* Lahore: 1922.

Agricultural Development in Developing Countries—Comparative Experience. The Indian Society of Agricultural Economics. Bombay: Thacker & Co. 1972.

Dandekar V. M. and Rath, Nilkanth. *Poverty in India.* Bombay: Indian School of Political Economy, 1971.

Darling, Sir Malcolm. *The Punjab Peasant, In Prosperity and Debt.* London: Oxford University Press, 1947.

Dasgupta, Biplab. "India's Green Revolution." *Economic and Political Weekly.* Annual Number, February 1977.

Datta, Bhabatosh. "Perspectives for Fiscal Policy." *Economic and Political Weekly.* March 6, 1976.

Finucane. *Report on the Cultivation and Trade of Wheat in India.* Calcutta, 1886.

Frankel, Francine, R. *India's Green Revolution.* Princeton, N. J.: Princeton University Press, 1971.

Frykenberg, Robert Eric, ed. *Land Control and Social Structure in Indian History.* Madison: University of Wisconsin Press, 1969.

Ganguli, Birendranath. *Trends of Agriculture and Population in the Ganges Valley.* London: Methuen, 1938.

Griffin, Keith. *The Political Economy of Agrarian Change.* Cambridge: Harvard University Press, 1974.

Hajra, S. *Bihar and Punjab, A Study in Regional Economic Disparity.* New Delhi: Economic and Scientific Research Foundation. June, 1973.

Hanson, A. H. *The Process of Planning: A Study of India's Five-Year Plans 1950–1964.* New York and London: Oxford University Press, 1966.

Hayami, Yujiro, and Ruttan, Vernon W. *Agricultural De-*

velopment: An International Perspective. Baltimore: Johns Hopkins University Press, 1971

Hopper, David, W. "The Promise of Abundance." In *Regional Seminar on Agriculture.* Manila: Asian Development Bank, 1969.

Howard, Albert and Gabrielle L. C. *Wheat in India.* India: Thacker, Spink & Co., 1909.

Howard, Albert. *Crop Production in India: A Critical Survey of its Problems.* London: Oxford University Press, 1924.

Januzzi, Tomasson. *Agrarian Crisis in India: The Case of Bihar.* Austin: University of Texas Press, 1974.

Johl, S. S. "Agricultural Taxation in a Developing Economy: A Case of India." *Indian Journal of Agricultural Economics,* vol. 27, no. 3. July-September 1972.

Johl S. S. and Mudahar, Mohinder S. *The Dynamics of Institutional Change and Rural Development in Punjab, India.* Center for International Studies. Ithaca, N.Y.: Cornell University, November 1974.

Krishna, Raj. "Intersectoral Equity and Agricultural Taxation in India." Paper presented at Conference on Strategies for Agricultural Development in the 1970s. Stanford, Calif.: Stanford University, 1971.

Lakdawala, D. T. "Is there a Case for Tax Reductions and Concessions?" *Economic and Political Weekly.* March 6, 1976.

Land Reform. World Bank Sector Policy Paper. Washington D.C.: May, 1975.

Leontief, Wassily. "Theoretical Assumptions and Nonobserved Facts," *The American Economic Review,* vol. 41, no. 1. March 1971.

Mackenna, James. *Agriculture in India.* Calcutta: Government Printing Press, 1915.

Mason, Edward S. *Economic Development in India and Pakistan.* Occasional Papers in International Affairs, no. 13. Cambridge: Harvard University, 1966.

Mathew, E. T. "Taxation of Agricultural Wealth and Income." *Economic and Political Weekly.* May 5, 1973.

Mellor, John W. *The New Economics of Growth: A Strategy for India and the Developing World.* Ithaca, N.Y.: Cornell University Press, 1976.

Merillat, H. C. L. *Land and the Constitution in India.* New York and London: Columbia University Press, 1970.

Metcalf, Thomas R. *Landlords without Land: The U.P. Zamindari Today.* South Asia Series, Institute of International Studies. Reprint no. 274. Berkeley: University of California, n.d.

Michie, Aruna Nayyar. "Structural Inequality and Agrarian Change." *Social Science Quarterly.* September, 1978.

Michie, Barry H. *Structure in Diversity: Variations in Productivity and Efficiency in Indian Agriculture.* Ph.D. dissertation, Department of Anthropology, Michigan State University, 1976.

Mukhopadhyay, Sudhin K. *Sources of Variation in Agricultural Productivity.* Delhi: Macmillan Company of India, 1976.

Myrdal, Gunnar. *Asian Drama: An Inquiry into the Poverty of Nations.* New York: Pantheon Press, 1968.

Nair, Kusum. *Blossoms in the Dust.* London: Gerald Duckworth; New York: Praeger, 1961.

Nair, Kusum. *The Lonely Furrow: Farming in the United States, Japan, and India.* Ann Arbor, Mich.: The University of Michigan Press, 1969.

Narain, Dharm. *The Impact of Price Movements on Areas Under Selected Crops in India, 1900–39.* London: Cambridge University Press, 1965.

Nash, Manning, ed. *Essays on Economic Development and Cultural Change in Honor of Bert F. Hoselitz.* Economic Development and Cultural Change, vol. 25, Sup. 1977. Chicago: The University of Chicago Press, 1977.

Nanavati, M. B. and Anjaria, J. J. *The Indian Rural Problem.* Bombay: Vora and Co., 1951.

Pathak, R. P., Ganapathy, K. R. and Sarma, Y. U. K., "Shifts in Pattern of Asset-Holdings of Rural Households, 1961–62 to 1971–72." *Economic and Political Weekly.* March 19, 1977.

Raj, K. N. *Indian Economic Growth: Performance and Prospects.* New Delhi: Allied Publishers, 1965.

Randhawa, M. S. *Green Revolution, A Case Study of Punjab.* Delhi: Vikas Publishing House, 1974.

Rao, C. H. Hanumantha. "Growth of Agriculture in the Punjab During the Decade 1952–62." *Indian Journal of Agricultural Economics,* vol. 20, no. 3. July-September, 1965.

Rao, V. M. "Land Transfers in Rural Communities." *Economic and Political Weekly,* Review of Agriculture. September 1972:

Rath, Nilkanth and Patvardhan, V. S. *Impact of Assistance Under P.L. 480 on Indian Economy*. Poona: Gokhale Institute of Politics and Economics, 1967.

Report of the Congress Agrarian Reforms Committee. New Delhi: All-India Congress Committee, 1949.

Report of the Indian Irrigation Commission 1901–3. India: Office of the Superintendent of Government of Printing, 1903.

Report of the United Provinces Zamindari Abolition Committee, Vol. 1. Allahabad, 1948.

Rudra, Ashok, Majid, A. and Talib, B. D. "Big Farmers of Punjab: Some Preliminary Findings of a Sample Survey." *Economic and Political Weekly*. September 27, 1969.

Rudra, Ashok. "Big Farmers of Punjab: Second Instalment of Results." *Economic and Political Weekly*. December 24, 1969.

Schultz, Theodore, W. *Transforming Traditional Agriculture*. New Haven: Yale University Press, 1964.

Sen, B. "Capital Inputs in Punjab Agriculture, 1950–51 to 1964–65." *Economic and Political Weekly*. December 26, 1970.

Sen, Sudhir. *A Richer Harvest*. New Delhi: Tata McGraw-Hill, 1974.

Sen, Sudhir. *Reaping the Green Revolution*. New Delhi: Tata McGraw-Hill, 1975.

Shastri, C. P. "Investment of Farm and Capital Formation in Agriculture with Particular Reference to Bihar." *Indian Journal of Agricultural Economics*, vol. 20, no. 1. January-March, 1965.

Singh, Baljit and Misra, Shridhar. *A Study of Land Reforms in Uttar Pradesh*. Honolulu: East-West Center Press, 1965.

Singh, Tarlok. *India's Development Experience*. Delhi: Macmillan India, 1974.

Singh, Tarlok. *Poverty and Social Change*. 2d ed. Westport, Conn.: Greenwood Press, 1975.

Singh, Tarlok. *Towards an Integrated Society*. Westport, Conn.: Greenwood Press, 1969.

Smith, Adam. *The Wealth of Nations*. Edited by Edwin Cannan. Chicago: University of Chicago Press, 1976.

Srinivasan, T. N. and Bardhan, P. K. *Poverty and Income Distribution in India*. Calcutta: Statistical Publishing Society, 1974.

Streeter, Caroll P. *A Partnership to Improve Food Production in India*. New York: December 1969.

Streeten, Paul, and Lipton, Michael, eds. *The Crisis of Indian Planning*. London—New York: Oxford University Press, 1968.

Subramaniam, C. *India of My Dreams*. Bombay: Orient Longmans, 1972.

Taylor, Carl C. et al. *India's Roots of Democracy*. Bombay: Orient Longmans, 1965.

The Assault on World Poverty. A World Bank Publication. Baltimore: Johns Hopkins University Press, 1975.

The Royal Commission on Agriculture in India. Bombay: The Government Central Press, 1928.

Thorburn, S. S. *Mussalmans and Money-lenders in the Punjab*. William Blackwood and Sons, 1886.

Thorner, Daniel. *The Agrarian Prospect in India*. 2d ed. New Delhi: Allied Publishers, 1976.

Uphoff, Norman T. and Warren F. Ilchman, eds. *The Political Economy of Development*. Berkeley: University of California Press, 1972.

Walinsky, Louis J. ed. *Agrarian Reform as Unfinished Business; The Selected Papers of Wolf Ladejinsky*. New York: Oxford University Press, 1977.

Wilber, Charles K., ed. *The Political Economy of Development and Underdevelopment*. New York: Random House, 1973, 1979.

Yechuri, Sitaram. "Inter-State Variations in Agricultural Growth Rate, 1962 to 1974." *Economic and Political Weekly*. Review of Agriculture. December, 1976.

Publications of the Indian Government

Census of India, 1970–71. Delhi: Manager of Publications.

Ministry of Law. *Constitution of India*. Delhi: Manager of Publications, 1970.

Pocket Book of Population Statistics. Delhi: Office of the Registrar General, 1972.

Ministry of Agriculture and Irrigation. *All India Report on Agricultural Census, 1970–71*. Delhi: Manager of Publications.

Ministry of Agriculture and Irrigation. *Report of the National Commission on Agriculture*, part 15 (Agrarian Reforms). Mimeographed. New Delhi, 1976.

Ministry of Community Development and Cooperation. *Report on India's Food Crisis and Steps to Meet It*. Delhi: Manager of Publications, 1959.

Ministry of Finance. *Report of the Committee on Taxation of Agricultural Wealth and Income.* New Delhi, 1972.

Home Ministry, Research and Policy Division. *"The Causes and Nature of Current Agrarian Tensions."* Unpublished report, 1969.

Ministry of Irrigation and Power. *Report of the Irrigation Commission, 1972.* New Delhi: Manager of Publications.

National Commission on Agriculture. *Interim Report on Agricultural Price Policy.* Mimeographed. New Delhi, February, 1975.

Planning Commission. *Land Reforms in India.* Delhi: Manager of Publications, 1959.

Directorate of Economics and Statistics. *Agricultural Situation in India;* January 1966; August 1967; August 1968; August 1970; August 1972; August 1974. Delhi: Manager of Publications.

Directorate of Economics and Statistics. *Estimates of Area and Production of Crops in India;* 1970–71; 1971–72; 1972–73; 1973–74. Delhi: Manager of Publications.

Directorate of Economics and Statistics. *Food Situation in India, 1939–53.* Delhi: Manager of Publications, 1954.

Directorate of Economics and Statistics. *Indian Agriculture in Brief,* 9th Edition; 12th Edition; 14th Edition. Delhi: Manager of Publications, 1968, 1973, 1975.

Directorate of Economics and Statistics. *Regional Differences in the Growth of Crop Output in Punjab, 1952–53—1964–65.* Delhi: Manager of Publications, 1967.

Directorate of Economics and Statistics. *Wheat Statistics in India (Districtwise).* Delhi: Manager of Publications, 1972.

Economic Survey 1975–76. Delhi: Government of India Press, 1976.

Planning Commission. *First Five Year Plan.* New Delhi: Manager of Publications, 1952.

Review of the First Five Year Plan. New Delhi: Manager of Publications, 1957.

Second Five Year Plan. New Delhi: Government of India Press, 1956.

Third Five Year Plan. Delhi: Manager of Publications, 1962.

Fourth Five Year Plan, 1969–74. Delhi: Manager of Publications, 1970.

Draft Fifth Five Year Plan 1974–79. Vols. 1 and 2. Delhi: Manager of Publications, 1974.

Report of Steering Group on Fifth Five Year Plan Relating to Ag-

riculture, Irrigation and Allied Sectors. Mimeographed. New Delhi, 1973.

Report of the Working Group for the Formulation of Fifth Five Year Plan on Agriculture (Crop Husbandry). Mimeographed. New Delhi, n.d.

Report of the Task Force on Agrarian Relations. Mimeographed. New Delhi, 1973.

Index